LERWICK c 1900, described enticingly as "A Northern Venice" to early visitors who needed little encouragement to include some of Shetland's beautiful lacy knitting as essential souvenirs of their stay.

CONTENTS

Lerwick Lace Shawl ~ Introduction	page 1
Lerwick Lace Shawl Details	page 3
The Antique *Borders Inwards* Lerwick Lace Shawl	page 8
Edging	page 9
Straight Borders	page 10
Centre	page 12
Mitred *Borders Inwards* Method & Chart	page 13
Same But Different : My Sampler of the Antique	page 16
Outwards & Inwards Borders Comparison	page 17
An Alternative Edging for Shawl	page 18
Detail of the 1 Ply Sample – knitted '*Inwards*'	page 19
1 Ply Sample Border Chart	page 20
2 Ply *Borders Outwards* Lerwick Lace Shawl	page 22
Centre	page 25
Straight Borders	page 26
Edging - see page 9	
Mitred *Borders Outwards* Method & Chart	page 28
Appendix 1 : *'Running and Rooing'*	page 29
Appendix 2 : *Picturesque Life in Shetland* ~ *Extracts*	page 32
Appendix 3 : *"The Knitters"* by Eliza Edmonston	page 36
Some Knitting Advice including *Grafting & Dressing*	page 41
Chart Symbols, Knitting Tips and Aftercare	inside cover

I have named this antique shawl *The Lerwick Lace Shawl* in tribute to the many knitters that lived there and, by earning modest livelihoods, left us a lace knitting legacy.

"The finest Shetland wool which is very scarce, and every year becoming scarcer, is reserved for the very finest shawls and veils. Each district has its own speciality in the hosiery line. Thus Northmaven produces soft underclothing; Nesting, stockings; Walls and Sandsting, socks and haps (shoulder shawls); Whiteness and Weesdale, fancy coloured gloves; Lerwick, shawls and veils."

The Orkneys and Shetland: Their Past and Present State
John R. TUDOR, John Dunlop, Edinburgh 1883.

Please Note : Due to the intricacy of the lacework, this book is for the experienced knitter with a good understanding of charts.

THE LERWICK LACE SHAWL is one I'm very pleased to offer knitters, it is a direct interpretation of a Shetland shawl of about 1890 – 1910, shown left. Made of a fine hand-spun 2 ply wool, this came to me in rather a sorry state, with holes and weak areas. However, it was easy to see the high quality of its beautiful design.

A close examination of the shawl's construction showed that it had been knitted in a seemingly rather unplanned manner, for, where the borders joined the centre, there were a lot of erratically spaced groupings of multiple decreasings – see page 7. I first took this to mean that the knitter hadn't finally chosen her centre till the last moment and had done this radical reshaping then to allow for the new pattern. This I found actually both informative and reassuring : it showed that the knitter was so skilled she knew she could do this alteration - perhaps a decision on the spur of the moment when she'd finally chosen her centre - and that only a critically close study would reveal what, to some purists' eyes, would be less than perfectly mathematically correct knitting. (I surely couldn't be alone in being grateful for that!)

But finally I realised that though the above could still apply, importantly this gathering was most likely to be no expedient measure, but actually pre-planned : demonstrating a rarely mentioned method of shaping their fine lace borders that I now appreciate was used frequently in Shetland: a simpler **Cruciform** or **'straight sided borders'** way, see page 8. I concluded this as it is the third time I've met this solution in my small collection of antique Shetland lace, and so must prove that not all these shawls are the neatly regular mitred ones of books – a view confirmed by re-checking exhibits. I believe this simple advance could only have been used due to a thorough understanding of the unique nature of their wool's dressing qualities.

The more I studied this lovely shawl the more there was to learn from it and to absorb for future lace projects; so I intend it here to be the basis for a series of related designs that knitters can either work from directly; or, by referring to these examples, gain a clearer understanding of some of the calculations and considerations involved (such as yarn choice, construction method and shaping), so as to be more confident in their own design work.

Finally, any serious contemplation of antique Shetland Lace must include considering the woollen *'thread'** from which it was made, and any research into this leads one only to better appreciate the lives and methods involved in sheep-keeping and wool processing in those distant days of over a hundred years ago. Many interesting things of relevance can yet be gleaned from direct reference to 19th & early 20th century sources so to this end, I have added Appendices concerning 'Running and Rooing' Shetland sheep, an ancient, early farming practice that was widespread there until at least the 1950s; and some moving portrayals of Shetland knitters from the 1850s and late 1880s, which are both informative and poignant.

SHARON MILLER

* *'italic words'* like this are Shetland terms.

Lerwick Lace Shawl ~ Introduction

I give this quietly beautiful pattern in two main forms : a tidied up recreation of the antique, suitable for being made with **Shetland Supreme 1 Ply** and knitted in the traditional manner by being made *Borders Inwards*, so you start by knitting the **edging** first and finish with the **centre**. This 'more advanced skill level' shawl is made exactly as the original was made: with straight-sided/Cruciform borders, but for those that need it, I also give a 'mitred borders' version.

For the easier **Shetland Supreme 2 Ply** shawl, I switch methods and show the design made *Borders Outwards*. For this, you make the **centre** first and the **edging** last. Experienced knitters will know this method will normally need the use of a circular needle to minimize the sewing together finish (the traditional '*Inwards*' way involves rather tedious grafting of the top of the centre to its border).

So, the 2 Ply Grey shawl is knitted outwards and was made using a circular needle. As said, the centre square is worked first, then either the Cruciform or Mitred borders – charts for both shapes – are picked up from the sides, and knitted outwards: either all four borders at once, *'knitting in the round'* (**experienced method**); or each border can be made separately *'flat'*, (using regular straight needles) before these are sewn together ('**easiest of all' method**). To finish, the edging strip is knitted round the borders.

As will be seen (page 17), the switch between these two methods effectively inverts the border pattern order; an important design consideration. For the sake of interest, I have also introduced small changes in pattern in a sample (page 16) which I hope will show knitters some of the subtler changes that can be made and their consequences.

Experienced knitters will realise that whether the borders are made '*inwards*' or '*outwards*', the designs could be made in any of the following list of yarns. So, for example, a 1 Ply shawl could be made *Borders Outwards,* or a 2 Ply shawl may be made *Borders Inwards.* **Tension /Gauge** See also page 2:

Materials *Using Shetland Supreme :*

For shawl shown on page 22:

250g of 2 Ply
3.25 mm, 60 cm circular needle
 (**UK 10, US 3, 24 inches long**) or *needles for 'flat' knitting.*

For shawl shown on page 8:

150g of 1 Ply (includes approx. 25g extra allowance)
2.75 mm, 60 cm circular needle
 (**UK 12, US 2, 24 inches long**) or *needles for 'flat' knitting.*

Also, if 'knitting in the round': Contrast lengths of thread - 1 of one colour (A) and 3 of another (B), to mark the first and the three other corner stitches, or use stitch markers instead.

Tapestry Needle   Sharp Scissors
3 Stitch Holders *for 'Borders Inwards' method to hold border stitches while centre is made.*

Each dressed edging point = 2¼ inches / 5.5 cm wide
2¼ inches / 5.5 cm long
My antique shawl dressed to 64 inches / 160 cm square, but would've dressed a little larger if it were not so old. Its exact weight = 5.8 oz /162g*.

Recommended Alternatives:

2 Ply: Shetland Lace-weight 14 - 16 x 25g : You could try a swatch with 3.75mm needle, but this will give a larger shawl.

1 Ply : Shetland Cobweb 1 Ply 7 x 25g; or an equivalent in a range of colours: **Merino Lace** 9 x 25g* to allow for mitres.
Gossamer Merino 3 x 50g * - mitred corners (c.2mm needle).

Experts: For a really fine shawl, consider **CashSilk**: Swatch for chosen needle (1.5mm - 2mm range), allow 4 – 8 x 25g depending on mitring, effects with needle choice, and very likely, more pattern repeats to keep overall shawl size. You will need to decide more precise quantities for yourself as these are variables only you can decide. Start by knitting an edging to desired length and pick up stitches and work pattern *inwards* with any new full 'repeats of stitches' included.

*The minimum **Shetland Cobweb 1 Ply** to get should be 175g (7 x 25g) with 2.75mm needle : *But never knit projects with the nagging doubt you might not have enough yarn, the saving on yarn cost isn't worth the stress!*

But **Please Note** : *If substituting with **non-Shetland wool** such as Merino, please get in an additional 25% extra yarn to allow for the **mitred corners** (see pages 13 & 28) as you will be knitting the "yarn equivalent" of another straight border.*

Tension Guide using *Shetland Supreme*

Knit a GARTER STITCH BLOCK :

Lace Cast On for 40 stitches, knit 40 rows, Lace Cast Off – i.e. extremely stretchy. Undressed tension for both 1 Ply (2.75mm needle) & 2 Ply (3.25mm needle):

10 sts x 28 rows = 2 inches /5 cm*

For *more* stitches/rows per 2 ins/5 cm square, use a *smaller* needle.
For **less** stitches/rows per 2 ins/5 cm square, use a **larger** needle.

Shawls are not designed to fit, so a little more or less overall won't matter, just ensure you have enough wool.

Please read all the following directions through before starting, so you know which shawl method (e.g. *Borders Inwards*) you would like to follow for your shawl.

I had a lucky find when I bought this old shawl and was very pleased with certain new things I learnt from a study of it. I give an outline of its analysis now, so that knitters will know how I 'deconstructed' a knitted piece to gain a better understanding. The first thing I did was a careful check on its condition in order to do any necessary repairs. I then made high quality scans of all the 'elements' (centre, border & edging) and started charting up each of these patterns, noting their 'stitch' and 'row' repeats from the knitting. Once these were done and the shawl had been conserved by a gentle wash and dressing, I used the charts, notes and scans I'd made to recreate the shawl : first in the *2 Ply Shetland Supreme*, a new wool with the classic airy qualities of the traditional Shetland, so having the prized ability to hold its dressed shaping and drape into the elegant, full, warm and light folds that best display the patterning; matchless for this Shetland lacework in my view, (though I appreciate there will be knitters that want to use dyed yarns instead, so will give details and pointers for these).

The centre was easy to recreate and indeed modify, something I did for the 2 Ply Grey Shawl so that the centre could be a "multi-directional" pattern - worn in any of the 'four sides of the square' it could be put on. I did this because the original antique's centre was a directional design: needing to be worn with Tree motifs either 'up' or 'down', but the 2 Ply Grey can be worn with these horizontally – see page 22. I calculated how many stitches the centre would need to give a match to the antique shawl, then swatched for a suitable needle and started the centre in Grey 2 Ply. As it was being knitted, I charted the border as it was - *Inwards*, separately knitting up the "Fancy Web Diamonds" to get that new motif correct. Once the border was charted to match the original, I 'flipped it' on the computer's design programme and corrected this new version so that I could make *Borders Outwards* Charts for the 2 Ply Grey shawl. As mentioned in the Foreword, I was now surprised to see the almost total lack of side shaping the antique shawl had, and how the knitter had resolved this with serious groups of decreasing along the tops of the borders, then I realised the benefits of this method for Shetland wool use. This is important to note because if you intend to use a non–Shetland yarn you will need a fully shaped corner to be safe from the outer corners curling. To that end, I created Mitred *Borders Inwards* and *Outwards* charts : pages 14 & 28. Charting the original edging - page 9, caused more problems as the antique wool was quite felted and worn here, however, I eventually got a fair recreation of that and worked it round.

Once the *Outwards* shawl was done it was easy to reverse the working order of it to get the corrected *Borders Inwards* form, which I then double-checked with a sample swatch after making small changes to the patterns to get variations (a lacier centre pattern, a different edging, a modified border design). Finally, I did an exact repetition of the antique centre pattern chart to check its accuracy. I blocked that and used all these samples as the basis for the instructions here.

Lerwick Lace Shawl Details

It gets to be important to knitters with an interest in history to know precisely what an antique yarn looks like and how it compares with yarns of today, so these pictures should be useful.

Below is a near actual life-size detail, notice the uneven 'hand-spun' 2 ply yarn, with areas of tight and lax spinning and plying - a typical feature in almost all old Shetland lace I've seen; this feature is a useful point in identifying if a yarn is hand-spun or mill-spun. Next, we'll go on to examine the shawl in detail, area by area.

Above four modern 'mill-spun' natural yarns that are recommended for this design, three of Shetland wool and one a cashmere / silk blend. (Note how well the colour of the shawl has kept). From left to right they are:

Shetland **Cobweb 1 Ply: 1/14NM**; HK's **CashSilk: 2/58NM**; *Shetland Supreme* **1 Ply: 1/16NM** and lastly, the latter's **2 Ply: 2/16NM** – I used the Grey for my shawl. (Not shown: **Shetland Lace-weight 2/14NM** which would substitute for the Grey 2 Ply, 14 x 25g.)

The **CashSilk** is available in 11 shades. Other good choices for those who prefer Merino would be HK's **Gossamer Merino 2/48NM** for a fine 1 Ply equivalent, and Merino Lace 2/28NM 2 Ply for a 1 Ply equivalent in a range of dyed colours.

Here is a close-up of the antique centre pattern as it joins a side, you can see some of the erratically spaced single and double decreases. **Note**: Just below the centre is an old repair in a thicker 'mill-spun' wool – I left this mend alone as it isn't too disfiguring and is part of the shawl's history.

Below right is an exact sample of the Antique centre pattern in *Shetland Supreme* 1 Ply, which gives a filmier and slightly fluffier result. Right is the original, made with slightly thicker yarn than the 1 Ply *Supreme*, that is a fine hand-spun 2 ply. As said earlier, you can normally tell a hand-spun yarn from a mill-spun one because of inconsistencies in the plying, unlike the mill-spun repair yarn here (uniformly spiral) the hand-spun has areas where the 2 threads are not twisted, but can be seen to lie parallel. The original 2 ply yarn is very similar to **1 Ply Shetland Cobweb** wool in overall 'grist' (thickness) and smoothness. The *Shetland Supreme* 1 Ply is finer than it; the *Supreme* 2 Ply is slightly thicker.

Another thing to note is the original is not quite as fluffy as the modern *Supreme* wools. Sheep breeding since then and today's shearing / clipping rather than *'rooing'* (plucking the neck wool in summer when it is naturally shed) means that the length of each hair ('lock'/staple) can be less long by as much as 2 inches / 5 cm, as clipping not only leaves a shorter coat behind - can't have cold sheep! but also removes the tips of new wool that would have been shed in due time; the photograph on page 31, shows the tipped fleece of a *'roo'd'* sheep. This all means that now shorter fuzzier hairs are mill-spun in yarn, as distinct from the antique yarn which was made of selected and plucked then hand-spun lengths, and so had less short hair included, and, because the locks were longer, made a smoother yarn. Some differences between 'Classic' and 'Modern' Shetland sheep and their wools are explained in the Appendices.

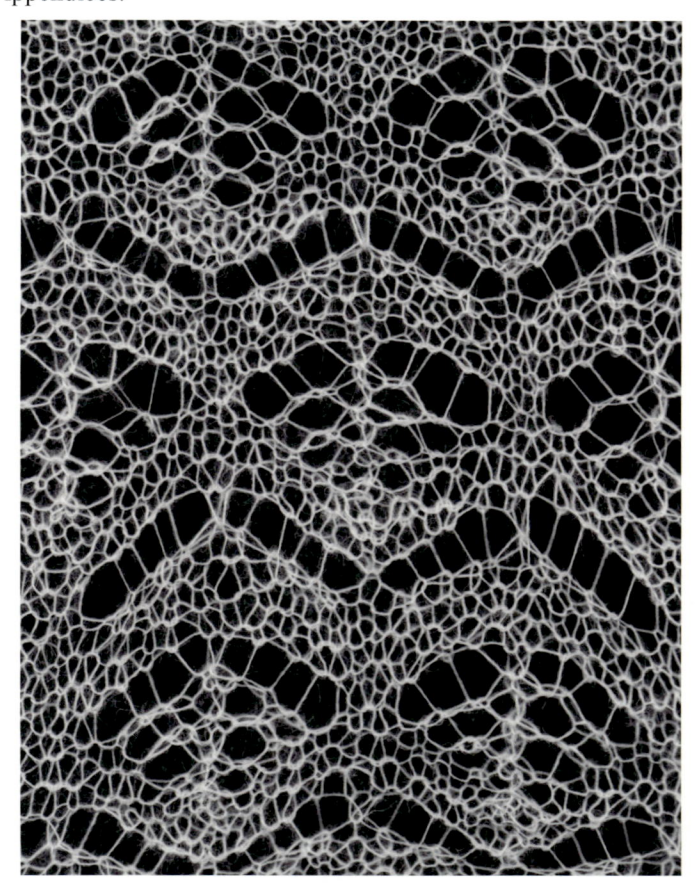

Antique centre pattern using 1 Ply *Supreme* & 2.75mm needle

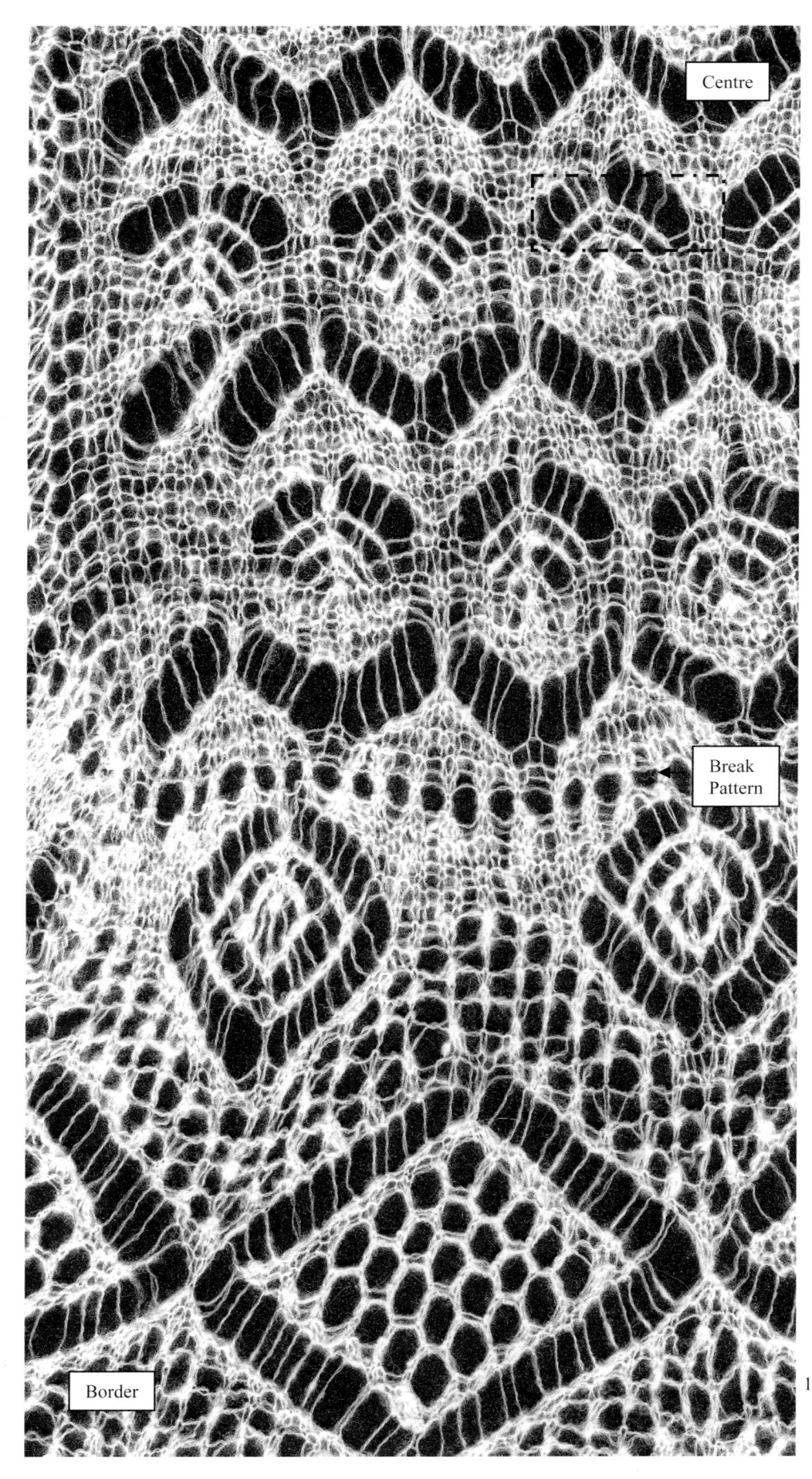

A centre corner of the antique shawl is shown left with details of the Centre and Break Pattern (with rather erratically spaced groupings of decreases for the Border tops in readiness for the centre).

The original shawl is made in a fine and now slightly felted, fragile 2 ply hand-spun about 2/28 NM (Shetland Cobweb 1/14NM 1 Ply equivalent) on what seemed a 2.75mm needle. I started by analysing the simplest of the elements, the Centre, a 20 row pattern:

To **get the number of rows for a repeat of a pattern** count the *'riggies'* - the ridges from one pattern repeat to the next and double the number :

10 ridges = 20 rows.

Check this in the detail below.

As the pattern is a typical-for-Shetland staggered design meaning the next 'block repeat' is offset, the pattern doesn't <u>exactly</u> repeat itself until **40 rows** are done.

To get the number of stitches for a pattern repeat count the wool strands (dotted outline, left) :

<u>**1**</u> **st** ('k3tog.') + (2 x 4 'make 1's each side of it = **8 sts**) + **3** plain sts = total of **12 sts.**

On the page opposite is my version of the centre using the *Supreme* 1 Ply yarn with a 2.75mm needle, chart page 12.

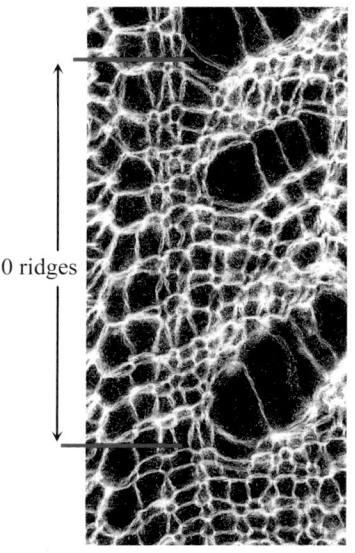

I started my study of the shawl by working out the simplest of the main patterned elements – the Centre. I counted the *ridges* to find out how many <u>rows</u>, and then the <u>stitch</u> strands there were for each pattern repeat, see right. A similar process went on with the Border and Edging. A significant change to the Border I made for my fine 1 Ply sample shown page 16, is that I put in more 'beads per zigzag rows' - the original border (next page) is like the one charted for the Grey 2 Ply Shawl, for a general idea **see overview, page 24.**

Original Fine Hand-spun 2 ply Border - compare this with my *Supreme* 1 Ply sample (page 19).
Dressed properly – something that can't now be done due to the relative fragility of the antique shawl* - the two borders with their edging lace would approximately equal the width of the centre. This is a typical Shetland apportioning of the elements seen in many of their traditional antique lace shawls: so that the centre is half the width of the finished shawl :

(Edged Border 1) ¼ + **(Centre)** ½ + *(Edged Border 3)* ¼ = **1** *(entire shawl width)*

* I can't answer for this shawl's handling over the 100 years – it must have had some neglect and rough treatment as well as treasuring. Despite this, it is still in a wonderful, useable condition, and shows that we can expect our knitted heirlooms to do at least as well with care. The knitter would be very pleased and proud to know her shawl is still here to do her credit.

Original Fine Hand-spun 2 ply Border Corner and Centre

Note the Break Pattern at the top of the borders with erratically spaced 'make ones' paired with 'k2 togs' / 'k3 togs'.

Here is a diagram of the antique Lerwick Lace Shawl showing the **32 lace Edging points per side**, **6 x (28 st) Border repeats** with the barest minimum of side shapings, and the **6½ full repeats of the Centre** pattern. This shawl was only decreased 'a stitch per side in the last 10 rows', I chart this as a 'stitch per side for the last 20 rows', as it's less extreme!

I cannot show in a simple diagram form the decrease/gathering by 30 sts that's done additionally at the top of each straight border ready for the **149 st x 276 row centre;** but this is a significant factor in the ability of the shawl to dress 'square' as it gives the fullness that is expanded into angles for the borders' corners. There's no reason why other knitters working with as forgiving a yarn such as Shetland wool for instance, couldn't adopt the same plan in designing new borders – just knit them straight and then decrease out a quarter of the stitches on the last rows (aim at 'a ¼' as you are actually decrease/gathering 30 + 20 = 50 sts per border which is ¼ of the 203 at the Border start). The great advantage with this practical strategy is that you needn't concern yourself with mitred patterning and matching of side-motifs; something that is honestly, a bit 'hit and miss' on separately made mitred borders knitted without a model or chart to hand. Shetlanders may well have been doing just this, judging from small mismatches in antique fully mitred pieces - which I believe is why the original knitters favoured this more reliable and less complex way of knitting lace borders.

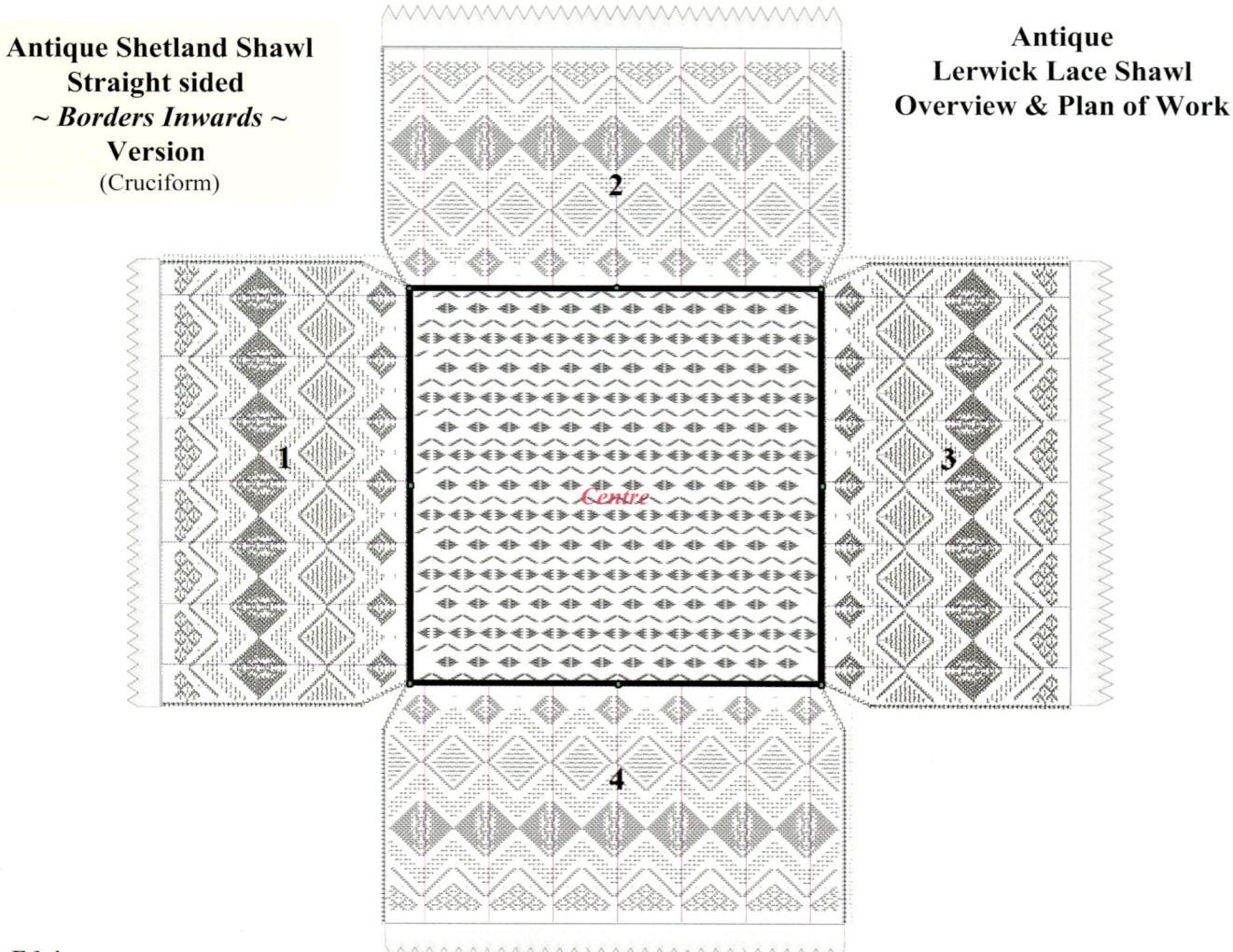

Antique Shetland Shawl Straight sided
~ Borders Inwards ~
Version
(Cruciform)

Antique Lerwick Lace Shawl Overview & Plan of Work

Edging
The antique original has 32* edging points a side: it's a 14 row edging pattern, meaning there's 7 'ridges' per point. So this means you can get '7 border sts per point' = 224 sts per side, but just 'pick up and knit' 222 sts. There's actually:
6 x 28 = 168 + 35 (19 LH + 16 RH) sts = 203 sts per side at start of a border.

so, if you are exactly recreating the original you'll now need to <u>decrease</u> by doing a row of
Knit 11, (k2tog., k9) 19 times, then finish: knit 2; this gets rid of **19 sts = 222 – 19 = 203 sts.**

***BUT Alternatively** and more simply, you can just knit **29** edging points and pick up 29 x 7 sts from them = **203 sts**. (SM : This makes me feel the knitter was doing what I often do, knitting something to approximate size before deciding finally the next element – the border in this case, then doing adjustments accordingly to fit.)

Borders
Knit as Border Charts, pages 10 & 11. At the end of Row 95 you should have
7 LH sts (6 x 28) + 4 RH sts = 179 sts.

To get **149 sts** at end of the Border ready for the Centre, finish with Decrease / Break Pattern 96th Row. Do not cast off, but save stitches on a thread or stitch holder. Make four matching edged borders. On the 4th, knit one of the **Centre** patterns as described on page 12 for 276 / 289 rows. Finish by sewing the shawl parts together and dressing.

Lerwick Lace Edging - original

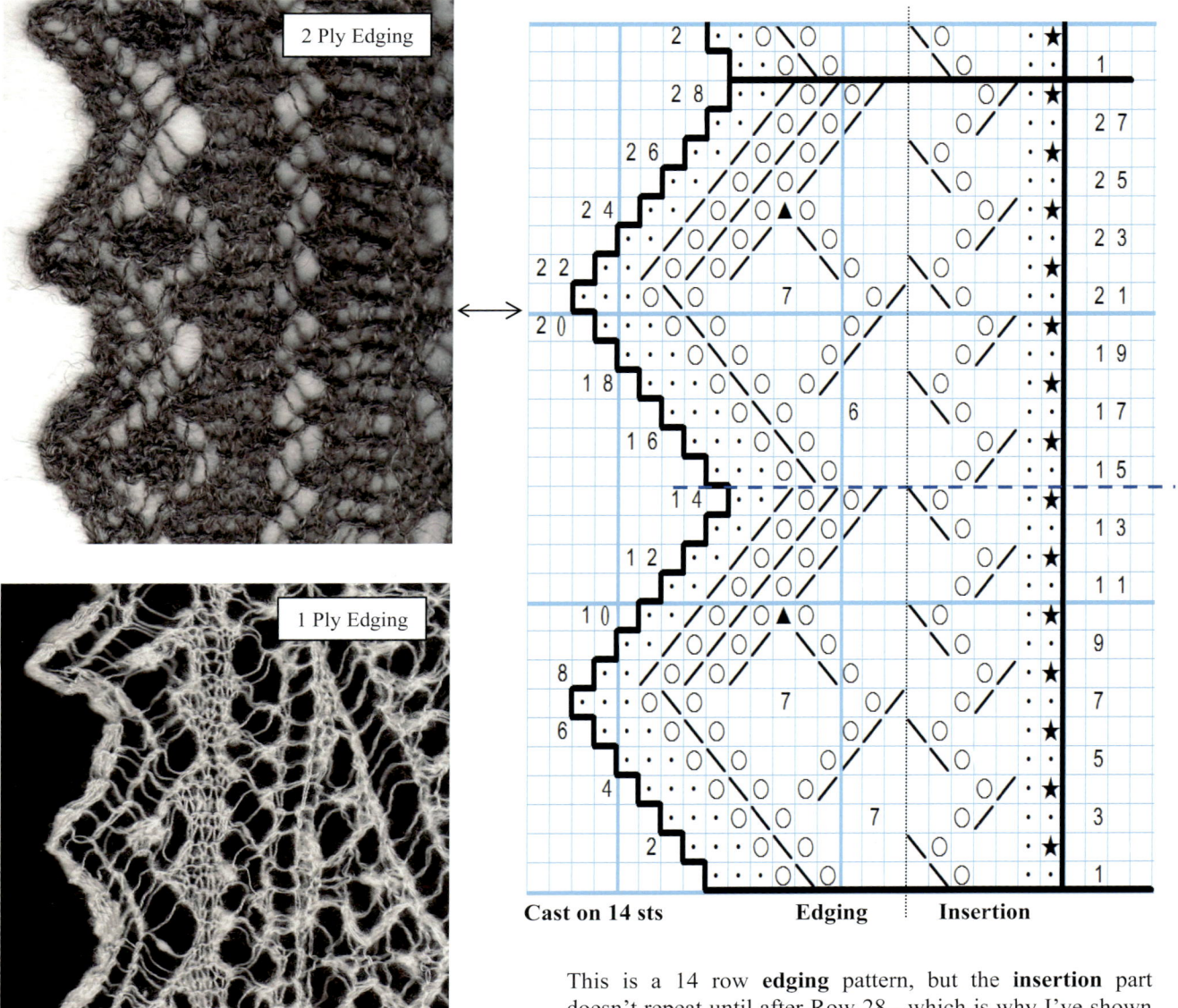

Cast on 14 sts — Edging : Insertion

This is a 14 row **edging** pattern, but the **insertion** part doesn't repeat until after Row 28 - which is why I've shown it like this here.

Star symbol = 'pick up stitch point' for border – so just knit this for knitting *Borders Inwards* method.

★ For *Borders Outwards* method, this stitch is treated differently – as a 'k2tog.' with next border stitch in turn.

The above charted version is as near as I want to get to the original antique white 1 ply one. That actually has a '3 plain stitch outer edge' (not just the '2' as charted above and worked for the grey); so if you want to do this add on an extra stitch and cast on **15 sts** and carry the extra one up the knitting at the outside edge - for very fine lace a thicker outer edge is a good idea. Because there is thicker yarn used for the 2 Ply, the Diamond motif appears wider than for the white 1 Ply, but there is also a wider plain area by the insertion. For a narrower plain area version that's more exactly like the original, try the smaller chart, right. Compare carefully these two charts to see how such tiny differences are charted and appear in knitted form.

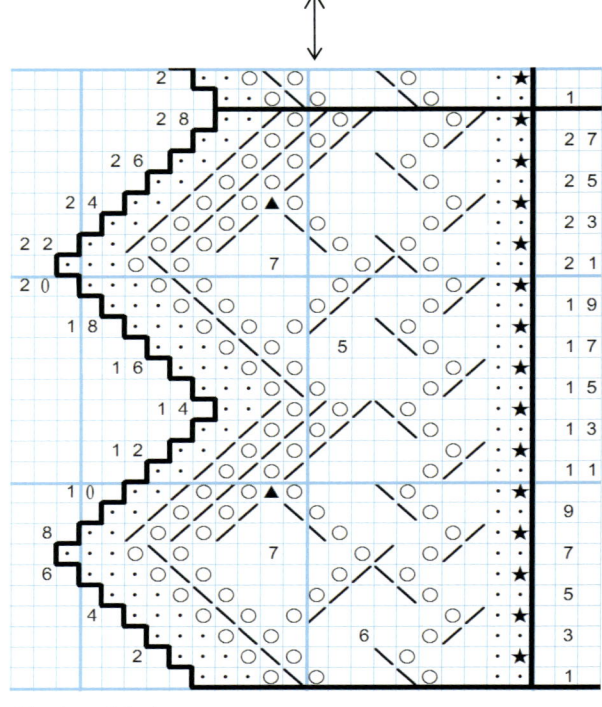

Use the Lace Cast On (or similar provisional cast on) for each of the edging strips and do lace grafting for their joins – see page 42. The antique shawl had grafted joins for the edgings, and oversewn seams.

Cast on 14 sts

≈ 9 ≈

Antique Lerwick Lace Shawl
~ as original ~ *Borders Inwards* Method – Chart 1

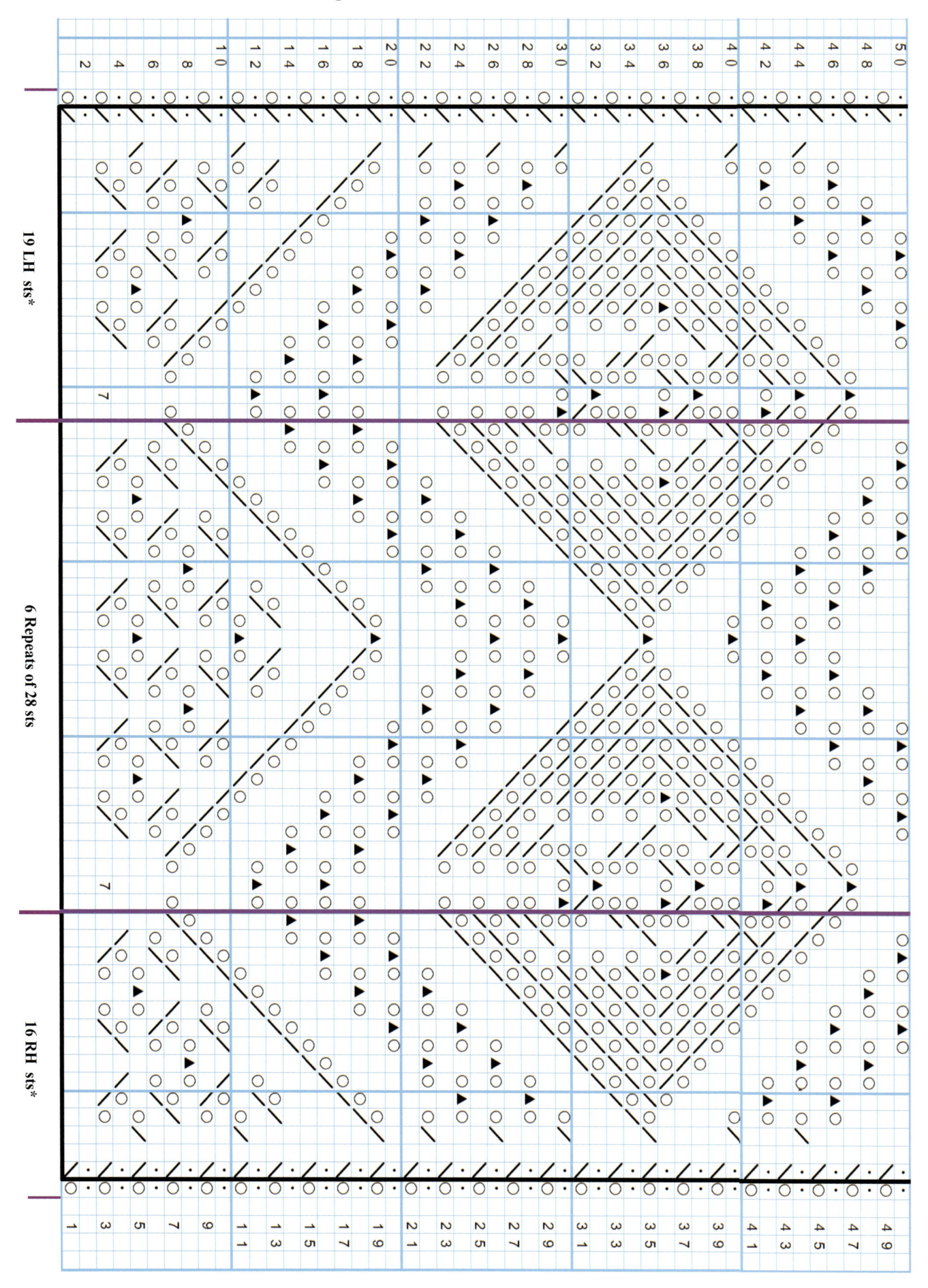

*Counting stitches just outside the black chart lines that define the border sides – the 'O's : Depending on knitter's choice, these can be made as charted (knitting in the round all 4 borders at once); **OR,** for flat knitting each border separately: the LH 'O/'s can be done at the start of every even row for an easier knit; **OR** these side stitches could be omitted entirely and the edges just knitted plain.

Antique Lerwick Lace Shawl
~ as original ~ *Borders Inwards* Method – Chart 2

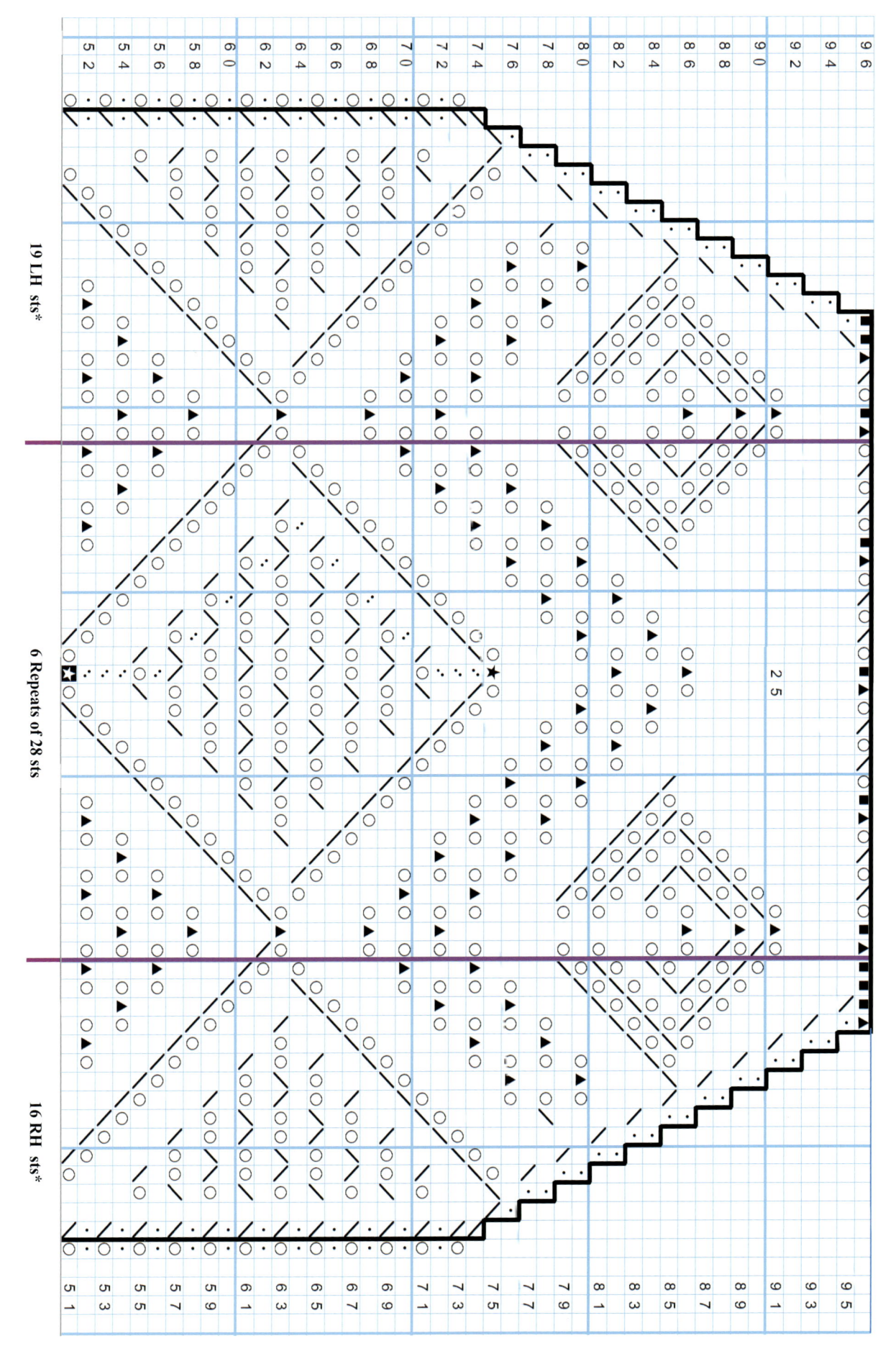

White star symbol = 'knit into front and back of st' to create an increase. This makes an extra stitch per motif which is carried up through each diamond motif and cancelled out by the **black star symbol** which here means 'knit 4tog.' These rows (51 – 75) therefore have **6** extra stitches per border. It's nice to do this as it makes the laceholes evenly centred in the diamond, otherwise, there'd be 3 plain stitches one side but only 2 the other. See note, page 17.

*See previous chart's note.

Once you've done this chart to Row 95, it's time to do the Break Pattern (Row 96) in readiness for the centre with its inbuilt decreasing ~ which takes down the top of the border by 30 sts to give <u>149 sts</u> for the centre.

⚜ 11 ⚜

Original Antique Lerwick Lace Centre

As shown on Page 4 ~ **149 sts x 276 rows** :

6 plain start rows (below Row 1**) + 6 x 40 pattern rows +**

finish Pattern Rows 1-29 again + 1 plain = 276 rows *(= 138 ridges to sew the border's 149 sts to on each side)*

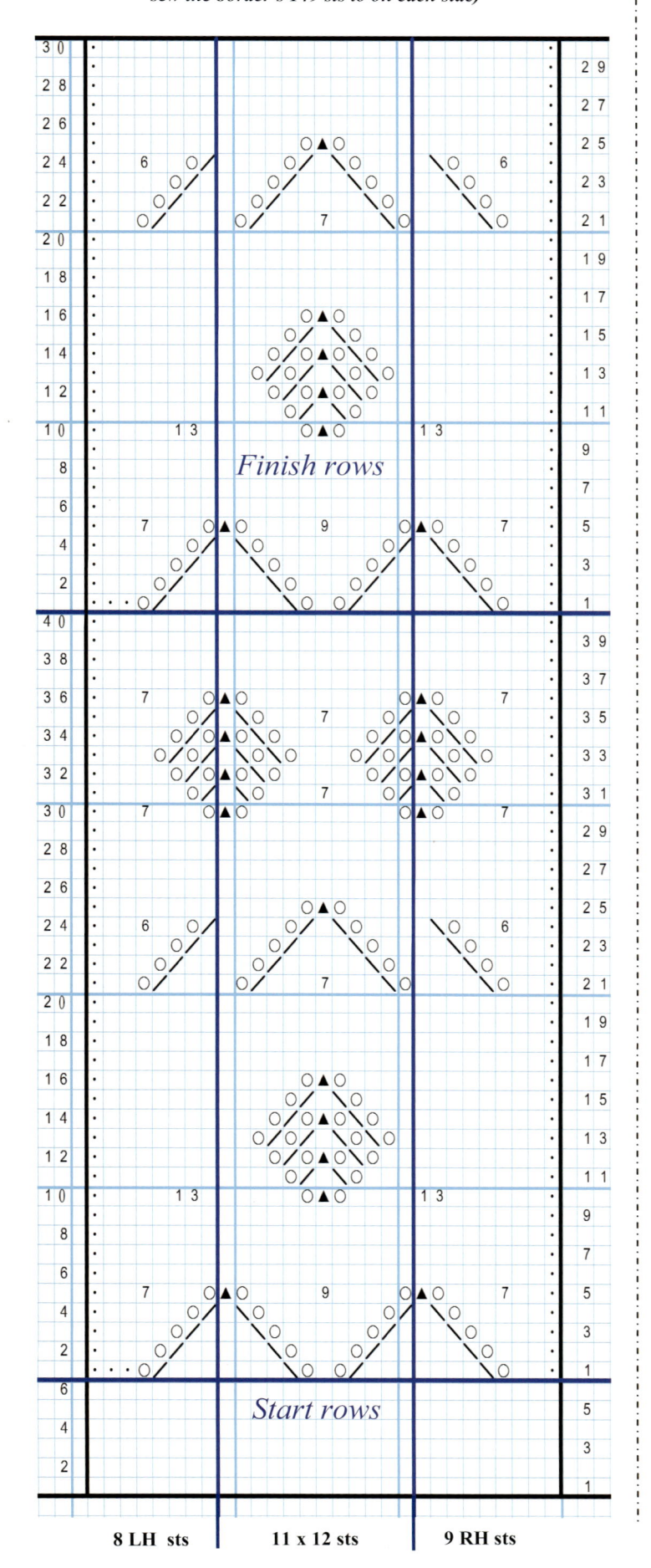

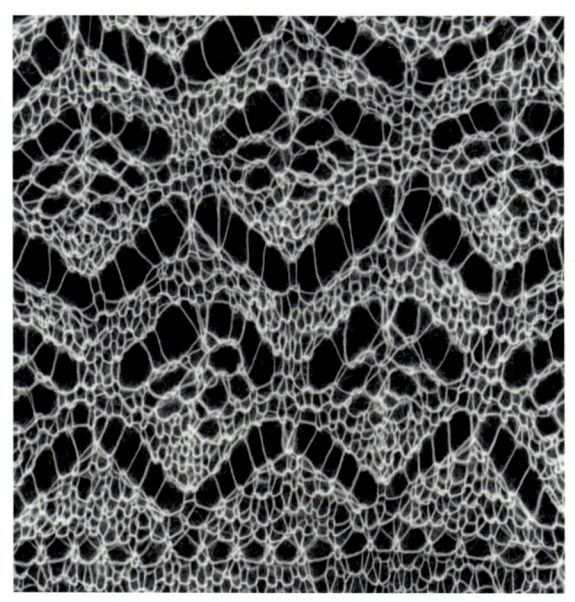

Shown above and charted below is a 16 row repeat lacier version of the antique pattern for a finer effect; worked with *Shetland Supreme* 1 Ply and 2.75mm needle. I created this by taking out 2 plain rows above and below each Tree motif of the original pattern, charted left. For this, there are still **149 sts**, but now **289 rows** :

6 plain start rows (below Row 1**) + 8 x 32 = 256 pattern rows + finish Pattern Rows 1 - 21 again + 6 more plain.** This actually gives a better figure than the original as there are now 144 *ridges* (page 42) to sew each of the two side borders' 149 sts to.

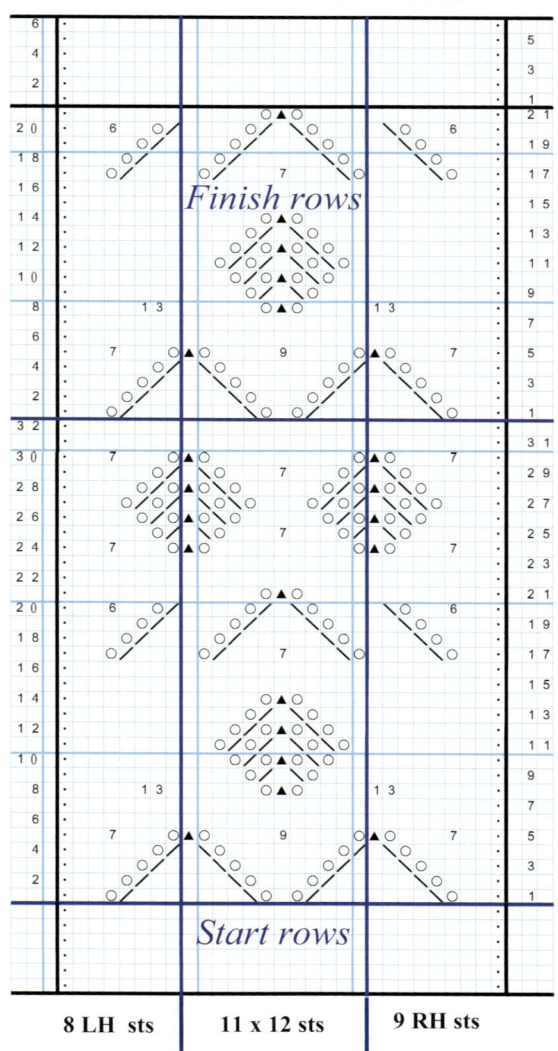

For knitters substituting Shetland wool or for those who prefer the look of a mitred shawl, here is a version that will work. Remember you'll need about ¼ **more yarn** than I quote for the original as you require **6 more edging points** and **2 more border widths** per side, see small green arrows on the bottom diagram which, with edgings, indicate this extra. So make:

32 + (2 x 3) 6 = **38 edging points per side**, then 'pick up and knit' 7 sts per point : **38 x 7 = 266 sts** as each border needs:

8 x 28 = 224 + 20 LH + 17 RH sts = 261 sts per side at start of border.

Decrease out 5 sts evenly on start of next row : start with **2 'k2togs'** and finish with **3 'k2togs'** to get **261** sts. Knit four borders as charted pages 14 & 15, then complete a centre as described on page 12.

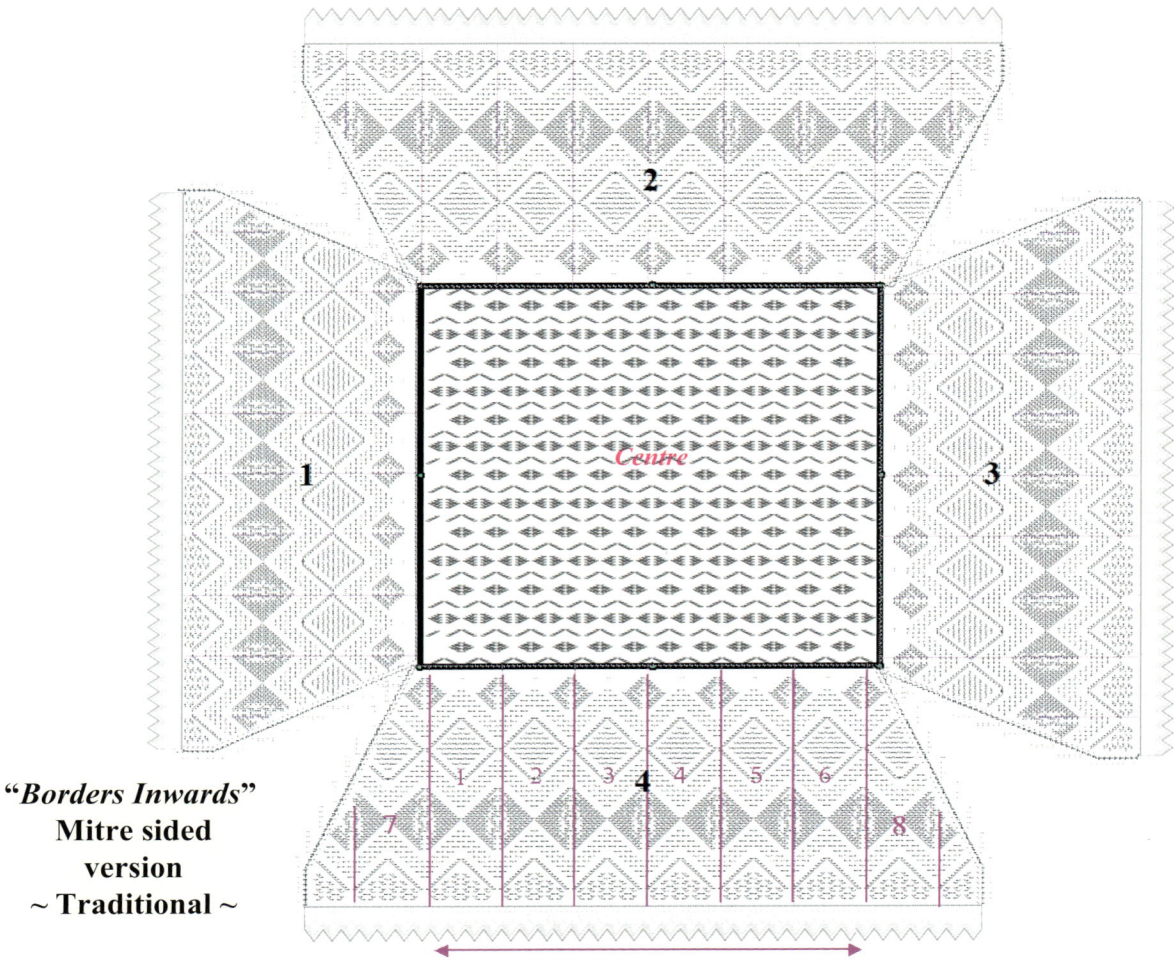

"Borders Inwards"
Mitre sided
version
~ Traditional ~

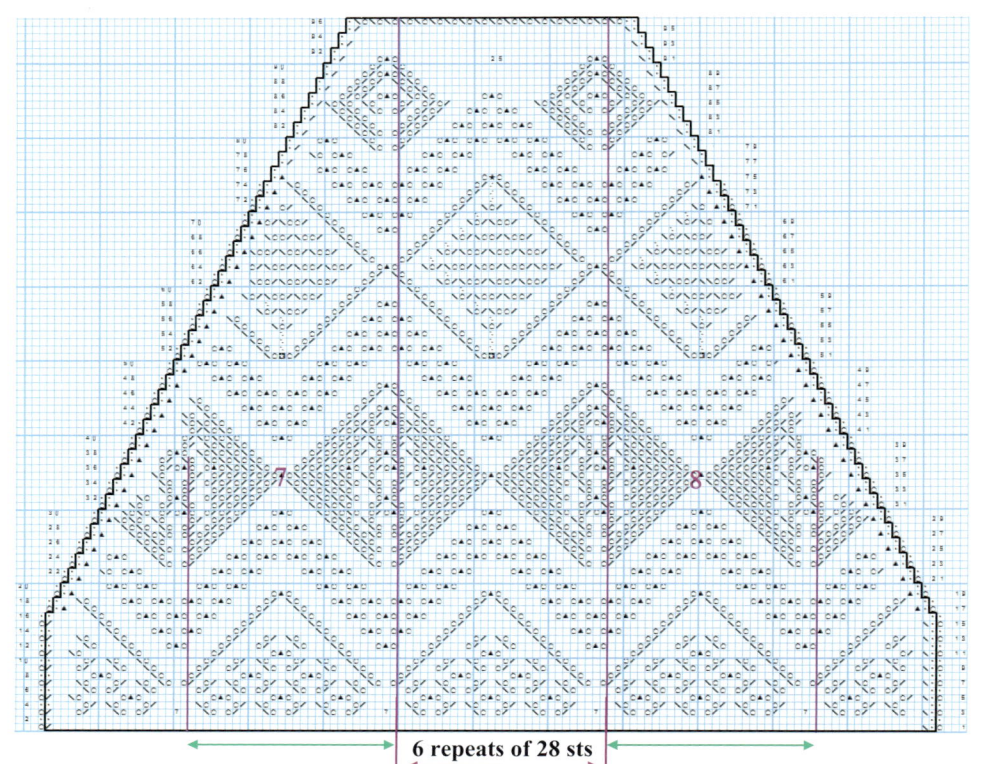

Here is an overview of the mitred border chart – the charts for this follows in four parts.

Although I mark in the pink bar lines that show the border 'repeats of 28 sts' on each of the four charts, **these lines change position** for Rows 38 – 70, and again from Row 71 to the end of border; to accommodate the shaping of the mitres – move any markers in your knitting to match.

For similar
"Borders Outwards"
Mitre sided
Chart ~
see page 28

6 repeats of 28 sts

Lerwick Lace Shawl Mitred *'Borders Inwards'* Method

Charts 1 & 2 : stitch count includes the 'make 1s' just outside pattern block at each side, marked by short pink lines.

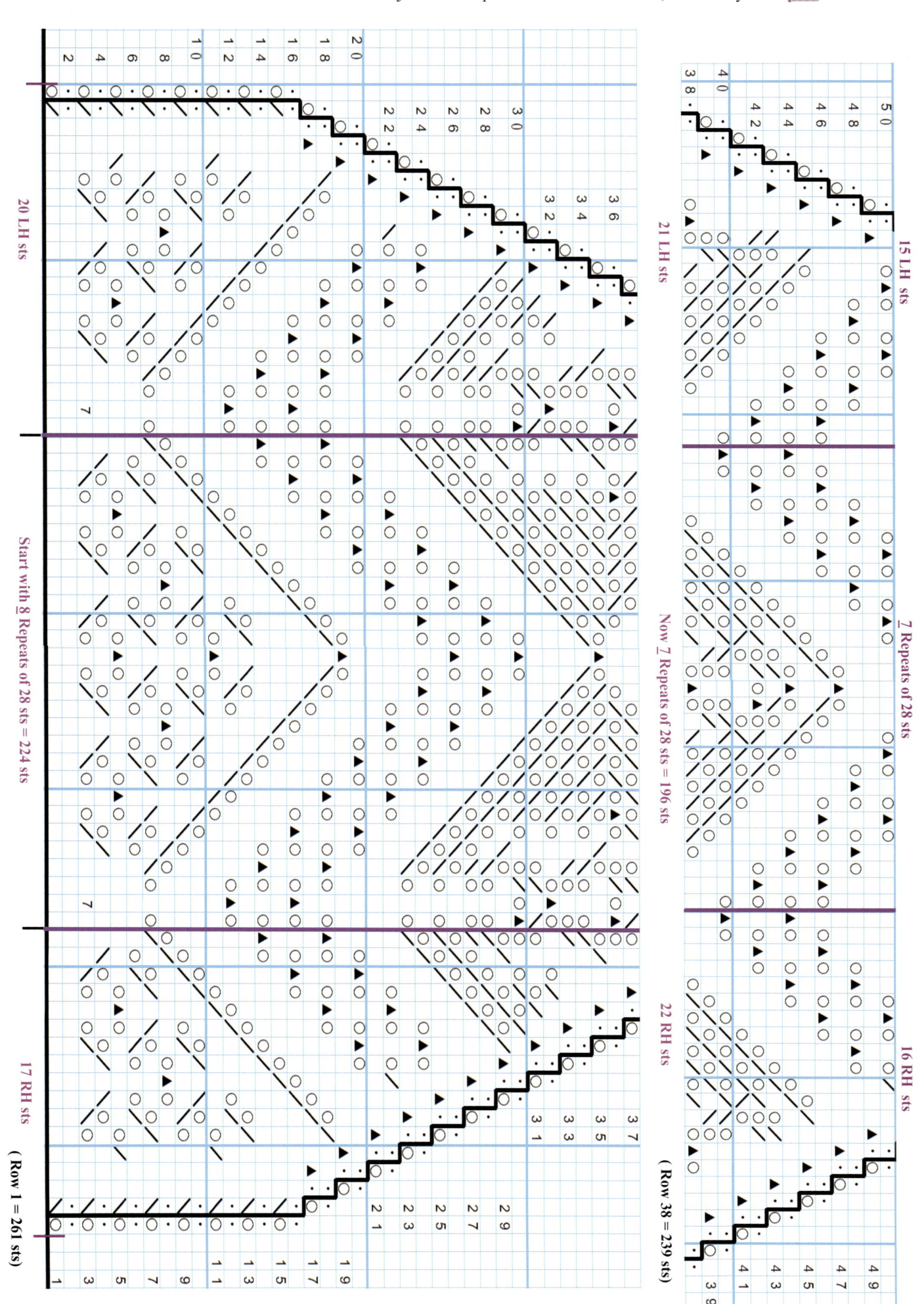

Lerwick Lace Shawl Mitred *'Borders Inwards'* Method

Charts 3 & 4 : At end of **Row 95**, you should have **7 LH sts + (6 x 28 = 168) + 4 RH sts = 179 sts.**

To get **149 sts** at end of each border (ready for the centre), finish with the decrease/gathering Break Pattern **96th Row**. Make four matching borders. On the 4th border, follow either of the **Centre** patterns – page 12, for **276 / 289** rows. Finish by sewing shawl together and dressing.

* '+ 1 extra stitch' per Lacehole Diamond made by 'white star' symbol.

Same But Different : My Sampler of the Antique

As mentioned on page 4, after knitting the 2 Ply Grey Shawl, I knitted this large *Inwards* sample for a shawl in the *Shetland Supreme* 1 Ply with a 2.75mm needle, as a double-check. I'd made slight variations to the border and centre for interest, and used another edging - one I'd seen on an antique shawl.

Once dressed, it was reassuring to confirm that this sample fitted exactly over a similar area in the antique shawl and the 2 Ply Grey Shawl, despite being made with a smaller needle: this unexpected finding again reinforces the importance of swatching to finalize needle choice. This border is charted on pages 20 – 21, the lacier centre is given left, page 12.

This edging has a double insertion – repeat part enclosed by dotted lines below. Single insertion edging shown page 18.

Assess your dressed sample from far away across the room (above right) as well as 'close to'.

This way you can get a better idea of the overall harmony of the motifs and elements and also, the density of these – whether the lace is too 'airy' or too 'tight'. Changing needle size will put density problems right.

Knitting a sample that include all your choices for a shawl is a good exercise and doesn't take more than a few days. Always dress and judge it from a distance as well as "up close", to see whether you like the overall effects. If something isn't quite right, it's easy to do the adjustments now, rather than rip out entire borders!

Star symbol – see Page 18

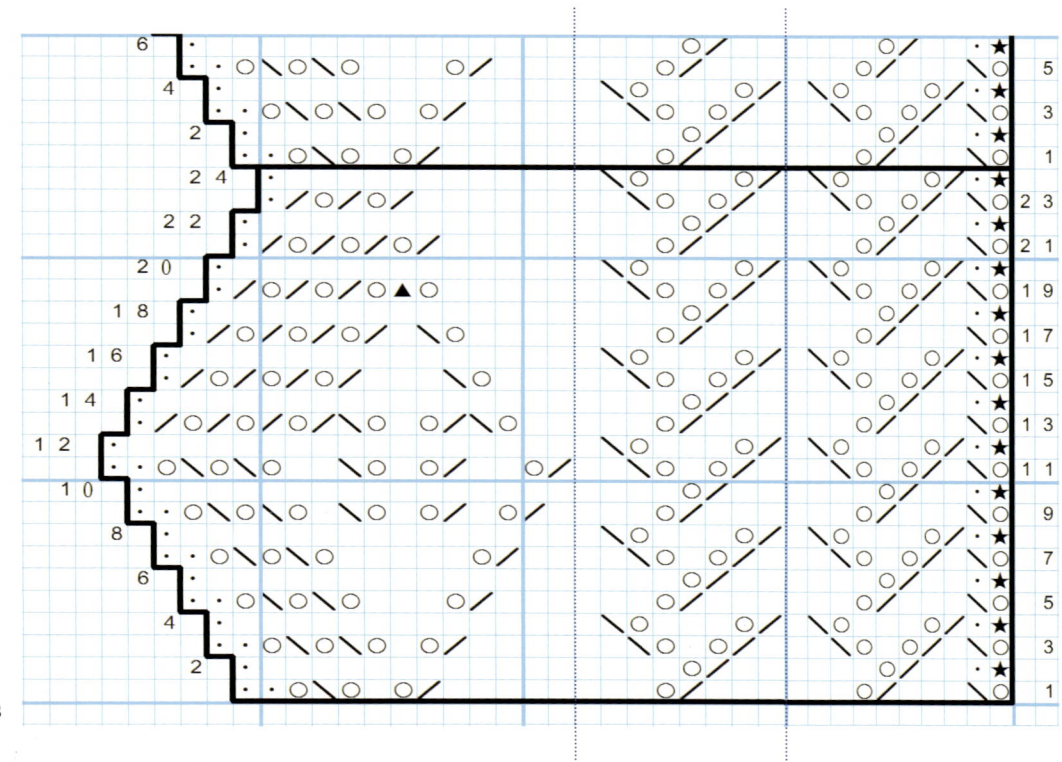

Cast on 30 sts

Borders *Inwards* & *Outwards* Methods: These 2 overviews of the borders show the differences between the two shawl borders that I've 'designed in' to make the border for the 2 Ply Grey Shawl (A) and the White 1 Ply Sample (B) slightly different and how subtle little changes can give pleasing results.

For the *Borders Inwards* version (B) : there are three pattern lines of 'O▲O' instead of the two in the *Outwards* (A), and no plain rows at the edging end to compensate. There are also very slight differences in the pattern – compare Row 3 of *Inwards* with Row 101 of *Outwards*. For the 2 Ply Shawl, I've tried to place as many of the pattern rows on the odd row side as possible to simplify garter stitch knitting in the round.

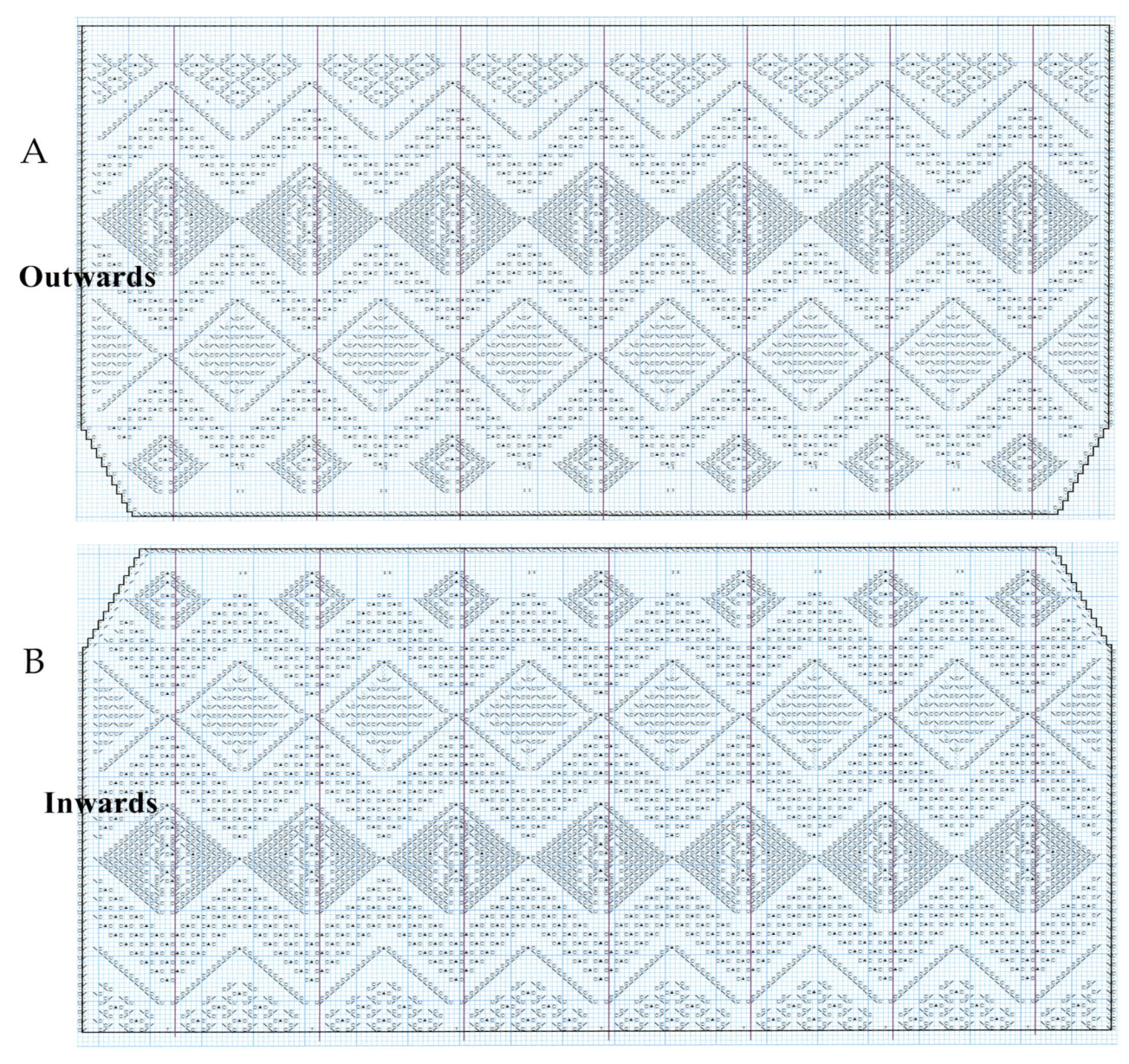

A **Outwards**

B **Inwards**

The Lacehole Diamond Motif

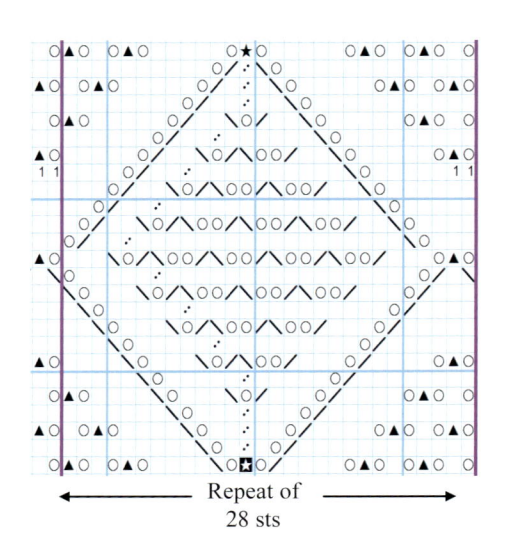

This motif charted as *left*, to fit the 28 st repeat of the border, actually should be 29 sts wide for symmetry – as *right*, and this is how it is worked:

An extra stitch is made at the start by the **'white star'** symbol ('knit into front and back of st') and carried up each motif. It is cancelled out by the **'black star'** (knit 4 tog.). The two **'black squares'** – *right*, mark 'no stitch'. The **'double knit dot'** symbols – *left*, mean make sure there are two stitches here, though the chart can only show one square.

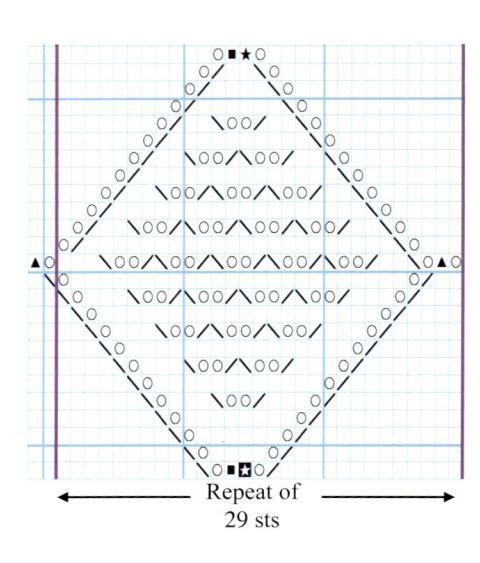

← Repeat of 28 sts →

← Repeat of 29 sts →

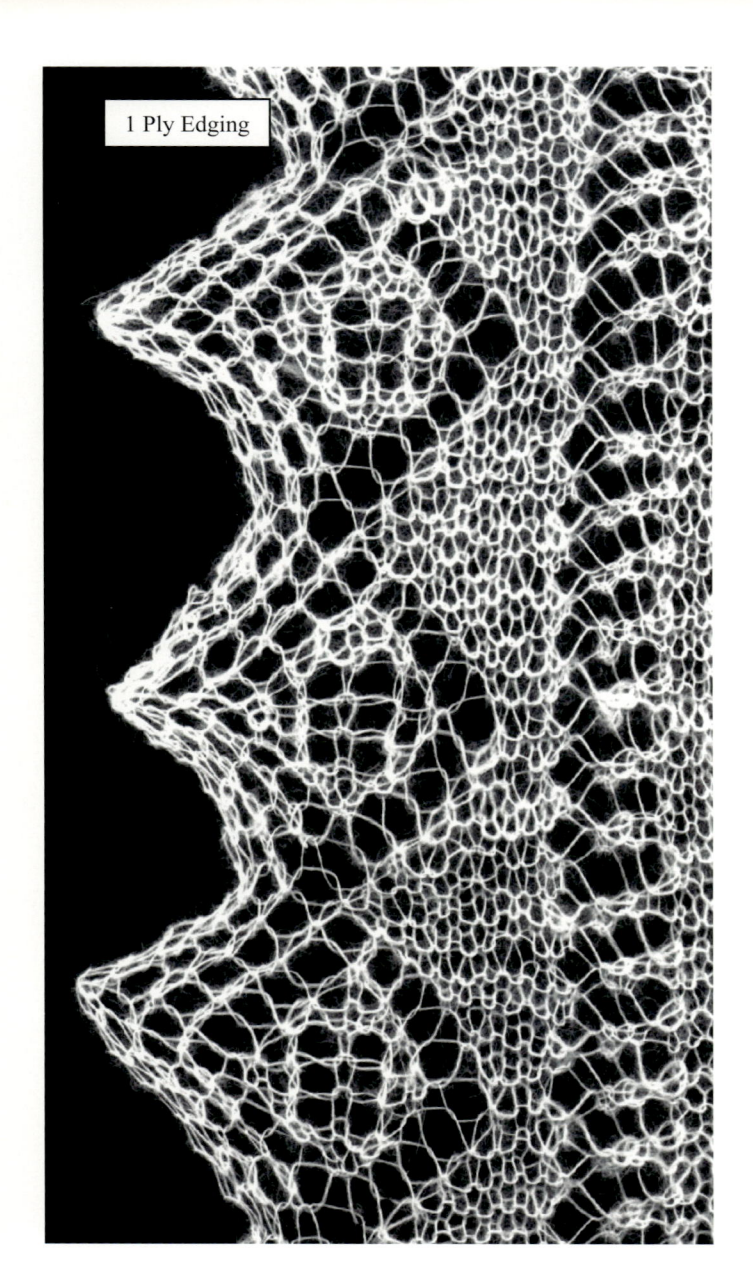

Lerwick Lace Shawl ~ An Alternative Edging

This is a larger alternative edging based on another antique Shetland one I used it as a foundation edging for the white 1 Ply sample, shown page 16.

I decided I might prefer the single insertion version rather than the double one shown on the sample, but it's easy enough to do the double insertion should you want a more pronounced line around the shawl.

This is a 24 row **edging** pattern, yielding (*Inwards*) or using up *(Outwards)* **12** border stitches per point, so would only need :

17 points per side for the 'straight sides' borders :
(17 x 12 = **204 sts**).

Or, **22 points per side** for the 'mitre – sided' ones :
(22 x 12 = **264 sts**).

Only slight changes to "stitch pickup" need making to get the **203** Straight / **261** Mitred number of border stitches.

Star Symbol = 'pick up stitch point' for border – so just knit this plain for knitting **Borders Inwards** method.

For **Borders Outwards** method, this stitch is treated differently – as a 'k2tog.' with next border stitch in turn.

Use a Lace Cast On for each of the four edging strips and do lace grafting for their joins – see page 42.

The antique shawl has grafted joins for the edgings, and oversewn seams.

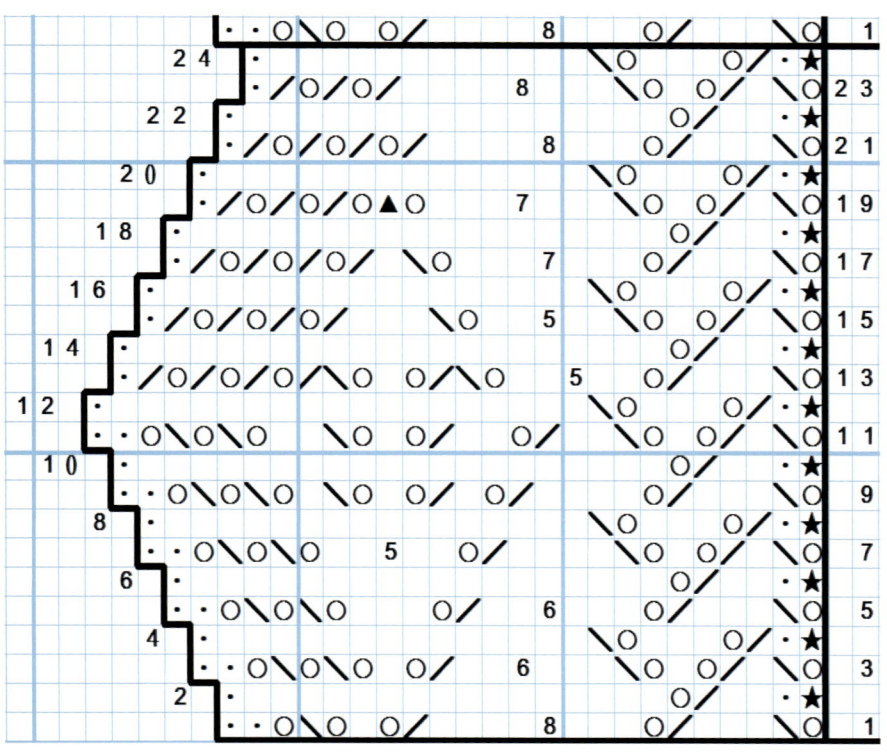

1 Ply Edging

Cast on 22 sts

Helpful Tip ! When Knitting an Edging around a *'Borders Outwards'* Shawl:

Wind a rubber band or put a toggle about 6ins/15cm in around the 'free end' of the circular needle so waiting border stitches can't drop off and you can still use its needle arm to knit with.

Below, there's also a red stitch stopper on the other arm of this circular needle – *no* stitches are escaping either side!

Break pattern →

Web Diamonds

Strawberry Net Zigzag :
3 rows of these, instead of two - as on the antique shawl.

Lacehole Diamonds

Strawberry Net Zigzag – 3 rows

Fancy Web Diamonds

Strawberry Net Zigzag – 3 rows

Shetland 'Fancy Bead' Triangles

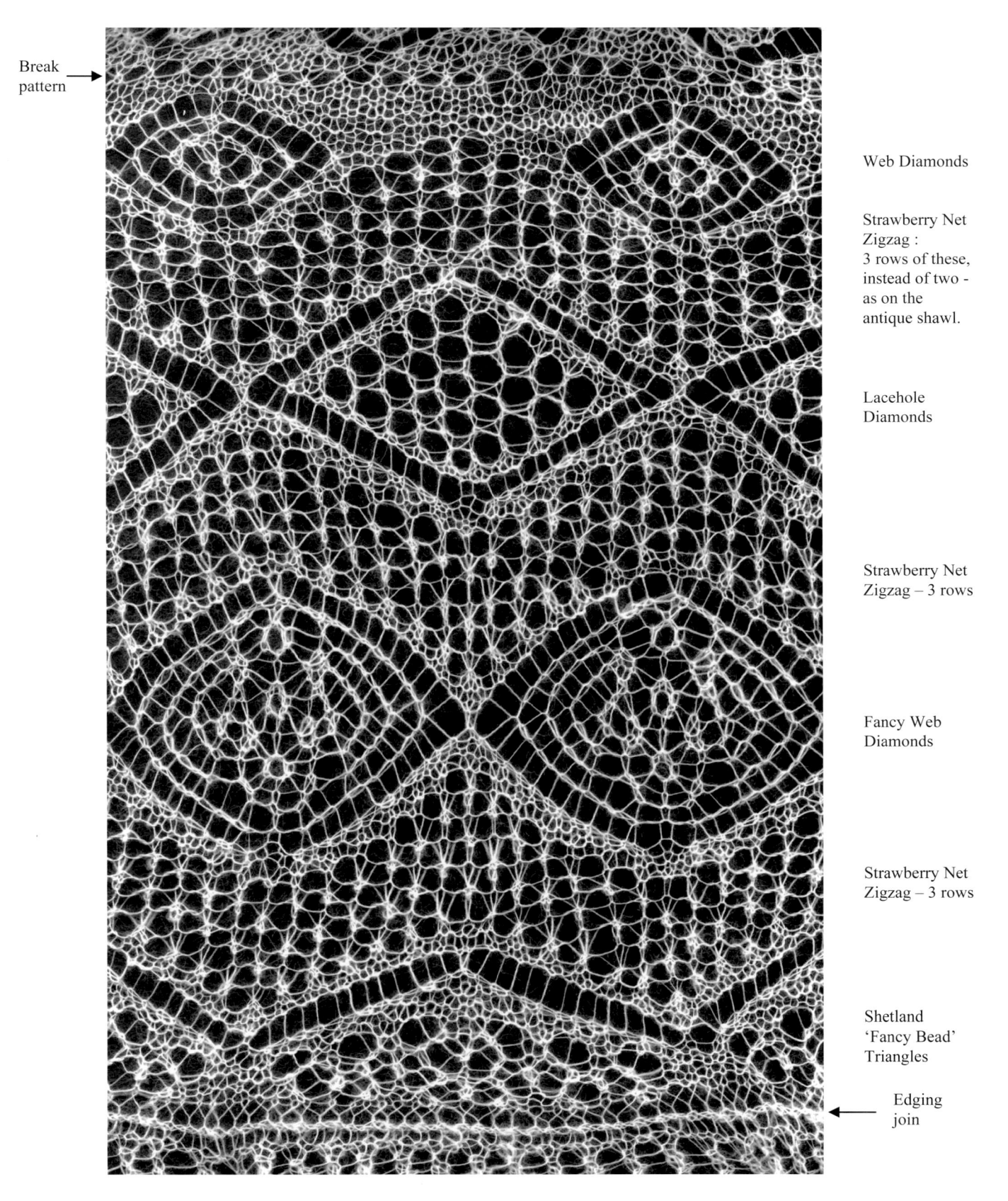

← Edging join

Detail of the 1 Ply *Shetland Supreme* Border Sample – knitted *'Inwards'*

This traditional Shetland lace border features a Strawberry Net background ('ground') with differing diamond motifs placed on the mesh. It is knitted up from the edging in the traditional manner, with the border stitches picked up and knitted *inwards* with minimal side shapings as the border joins the centre. The centre would be made on one of the four identical borders and the other three would be sewn onto it, with their pairs of adjacent side seams sewn up later.

This sample piece is very like the knitted original, and I was pleased to have worked out the Fancy Web Diamond motif – it was the first time I'd come across this interesting design. In charting, I've adjusted from above pictured sample very slightly in that I've put more pattern stitches in the plain area at the top of the 'Fancy Bead' triangles as they looked a bit empty here. An exact replica of the Antique Shawl would use the directional centre pattern shown to the left on page 12, and use the edging (page 9) I used for the Grey 2 Ply Shawl.

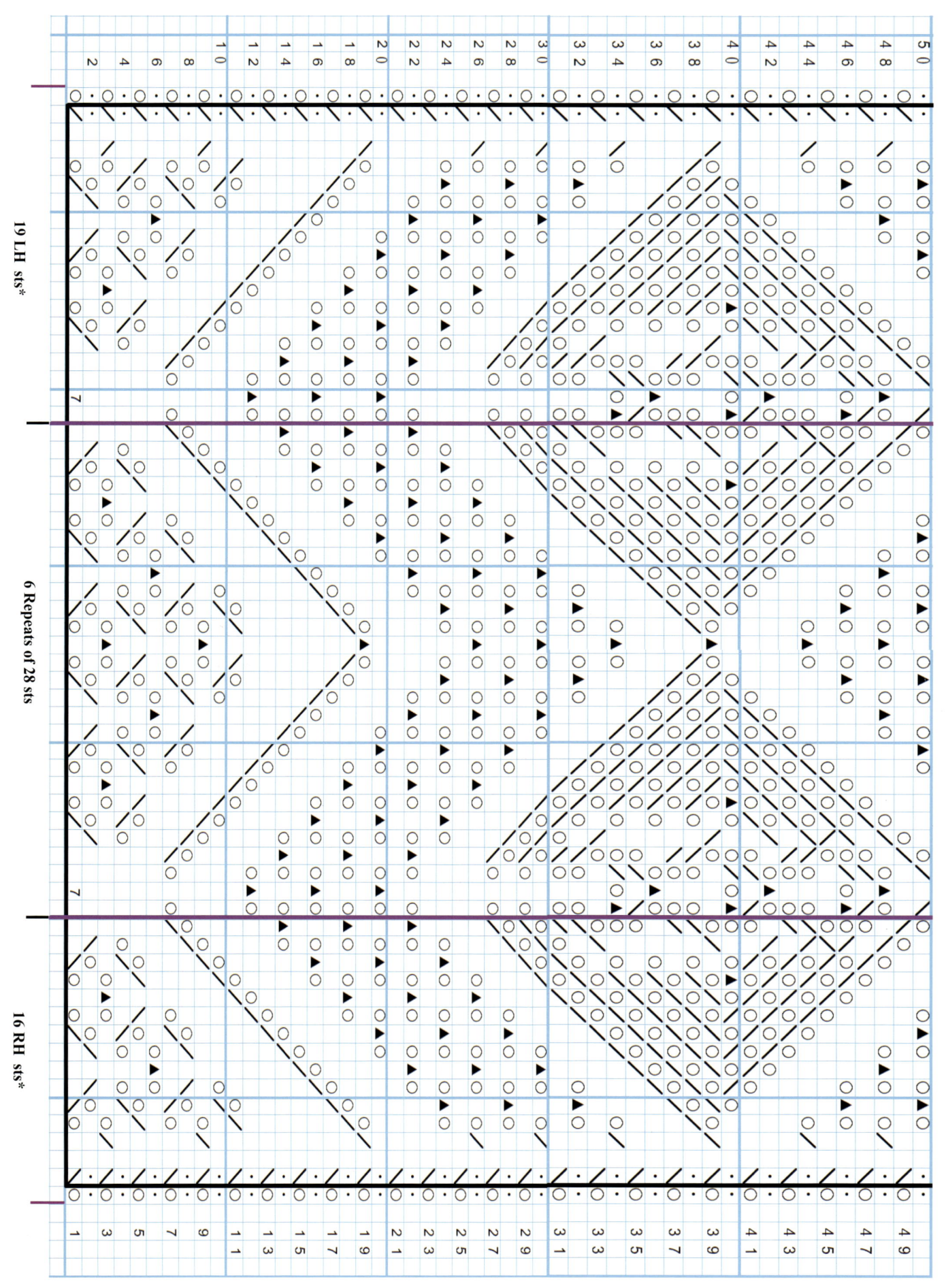

1 Ply Sample Border *Borders Inwards* Method – Chart 1

*Including stitches outside/just inside the black chart lines that define the border sides – the 'O/'s each side : Depending on knitter's preference, these can be made as charted (knitting in the round all 4 borders at once); **OR** for flat knitting each border separately: the LH 'O/'s can be done at the start of every even row for an easier knit; **OR** these stitches could be omitted entirely and the edges just knitted plain.

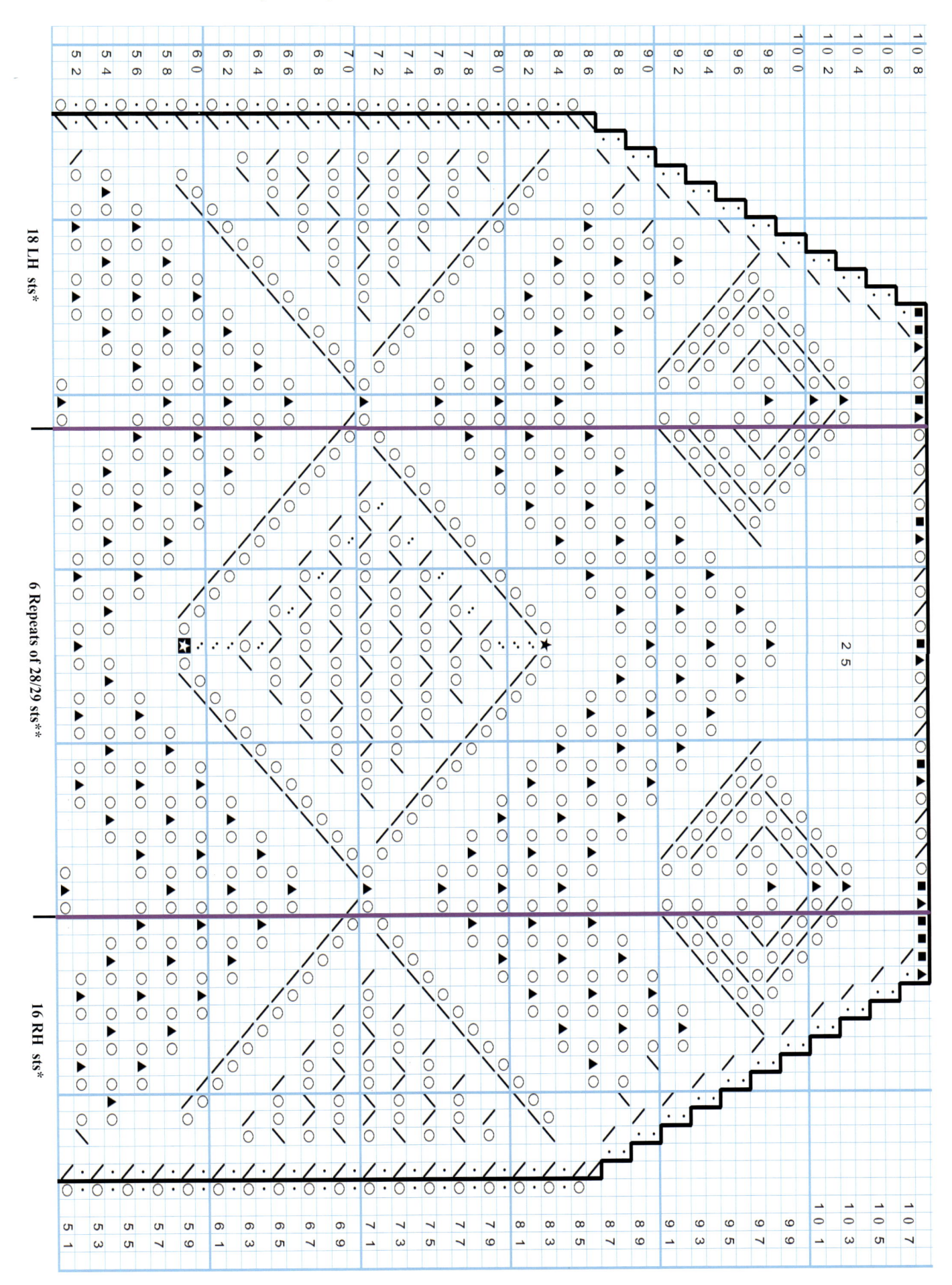

1 Ply Sample Border *Borders Inwards* Method – Chart 2

*See note with Chart 1.

White Star Symbol : 'Knit into front and back of this stitch' : To get a temporary extra stitch per repeat (29 sts) for this motif.

Black Star Symbol : 'Knit 4 together' : This gets rid of the 'extra stitch per repeat' created on Row 59, See note, page 17. Knit into front and purl into the back of each 'OO' on the following rows.

2 Ply *Borders Outwards* Version

This is an easier shawl to make as it is in a thicker wool and by being made *outwards*, doesn't need grafting. Experienced knitters can knit all the borders together 'in the round' purling pattern stitches on the even-numbered rows to maintain a garter stitched appearance.

If that is a little too challenging, you can make each border by separately knitting it from each side of the centre – this means you can knit the even rows' pattern stitches. At the end, loosely over sew each adjacent pair of the border sides' loops together, either before or after knitting the edging across the border stitches.

The borders for this shawl are knitted all together in the round, then the edging made around them.

These new pure *Shetland Supreme* wools are buttery to knit with and have wonderful warmth, lightness and drape, this is the feature that is especially linked to Shetland wool.

The centre for this Grey Shawl can be worn in any way and the Trees centre look well. If the antique white shawl was put on with the Trees horizontal as right, they'd lose symmetry as all the trees in that point would point one way.

The knitting direction for my 2 Ply Grey Shawl was *outwards* from the centre to the edge – as arrowed inset. When worn, the border actually appears as above (real size : 9 x 12 inches / 23 x 30 cm) and so the lace sequence is inverted or 'upside-down' to how it is when knitted. The samples shown here are in the stunning Shetland Black and Moorit 2 Ply, the shawl would be particularly striking in these colours in 1 ply.

Design Note: Inverting doesn't matter for these symmetrical diamonds, but <u>would</u> do with a feather or crown motif as these very directional designs would then appear upside down in the shawl when worn. Note the intriguing Fancy Web motif of three 'spiders' - or 'eyelids' / 'bird's eyes' - on a web, a pretty and inventive combination, see page 19.

Borders Outwards Method (Cruciform)

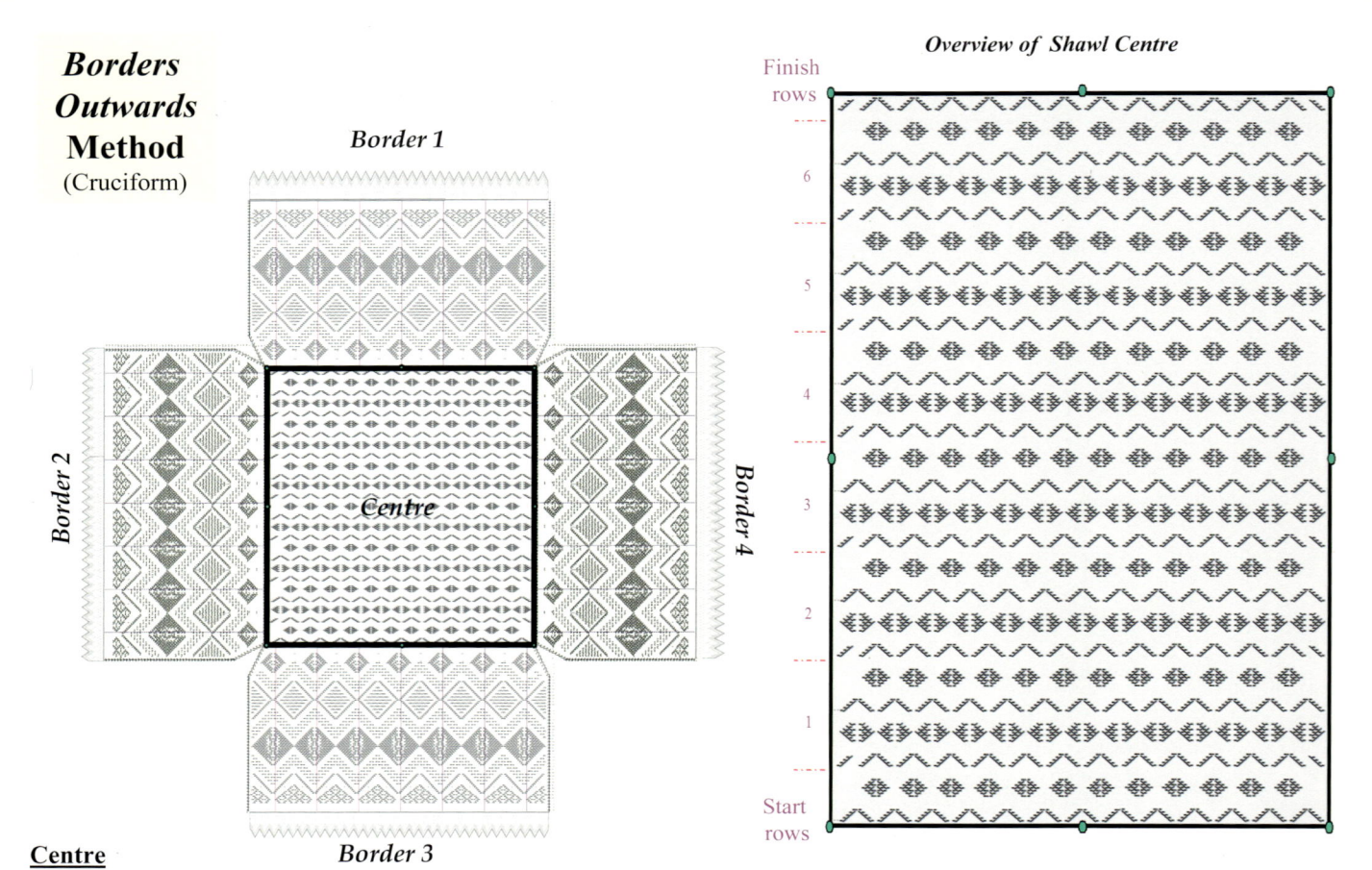

Overview of Shawl Centre

Centre

With this method you make the centre square first then pick up and knit from that the four borders outwards, and complete by knitting the edging around. Using an oddment of yarn, cast on **182 sts***: Knit the 182 back, then join in shawl yarn and **knit 6 plain rows**. Pattern Row 1: Decrease by 33 sts, as shown by Row 1 on page 25's chart, as this Centre needs **149 sts**:

8 LH sts + (12 sts x 11 = 132 sts) + 9 RH sts = 149 sts.

***Design Note** Method described next page. Although the centre has only 149 sts, it's necessary to do the gathering for Borders 1 & 3 <u>now</u> so each have **(6 x 28) + 13 = 181 sts**. This time, I chose to hide the decreases in the 'set up pattern' row for the centre instead of in the Break Pattern Rows for the border tops as done with the 'Borders Inwards' shawls earlier (shown page 11). Either gathering strategy works well; what wouldn't, is doing groups of decreases in rows of plain knitting <u>unless</u> these are exactly below a pattern row when the decreases would get 'lost' visually. You need '182' as, when you cut out the waste stitches you have 181 'loops'. A Border needs

8 LH sts + (15 sts x 11 = 165 sts) + 9 RH sts = 182 sts.

Next, work the decrease 20 Start Rows, then repeat Pattern Rows 1 – 40 six times (see diagram above), then work the increasing Finish Rows 1 – 10. **20 + [6 x 40] + 10 = 270** pattern rows in all. You'll finish with **181 sts** ready on needle for Border 1 knitting. Do not cast off, knit across the centre now as the first row of Border 1.

Total number of rows : 6 plain + 270 patterned & charted = 276 Rows : equals 138 garter stitch *ridges* down each side.

Borders and Edging 'Knitting in the round' Method (or you can just make each edged border individually if preferred.)

Each Border : 8 LH sts + (6 x 28 sts = 168 sts) + 5 RH sts = 181 sts. *All 4 borders : 4 x 181 = 724 sts at start.*

You already have the correct number for **Border 1** from the centre square's top and, when you've removed the Waste Wool Cast On, you should have the correct 181 sts for **Border 3**. For the two sides (**Borders 2 & 4**), you have the Centre's 276 Rows (which divided by 2) = 138 ridges. You'll regularly increase into 43 of these ridges to get **181 sts** for the sides. So:

'**Pick up and knit 1 st**' from each of the first **6** ridges, then:

*'Pick up and knit into <u>front and back</u> of next ridge (to get 2 sts)', then 'pick up and knit 1 st' from the next 2 ridges**. Repeat from * to ** 42 more times; then

'**Pick up and knit 1 stitch**' for the last **3** ridges :   6 + [129 + 43 new sts] + 3 sts = 181 sts.

Mark the **first stitch** and the **centre stitch** (the 91st) of each side (shown as 8 green dots on above diagram, right). Purl next round, then work as set out by the two border charts. Finally, knit the edging round (**29** or **32** points per side, see pages 27, 8 & 9) and finish the shawl by sewing the ends in and dressing.

Wave & Tree Centre for *'Borders Outwards'* Shawl

10 Finish Rows

6 x 40 Pattern Rows

20 Start Rows

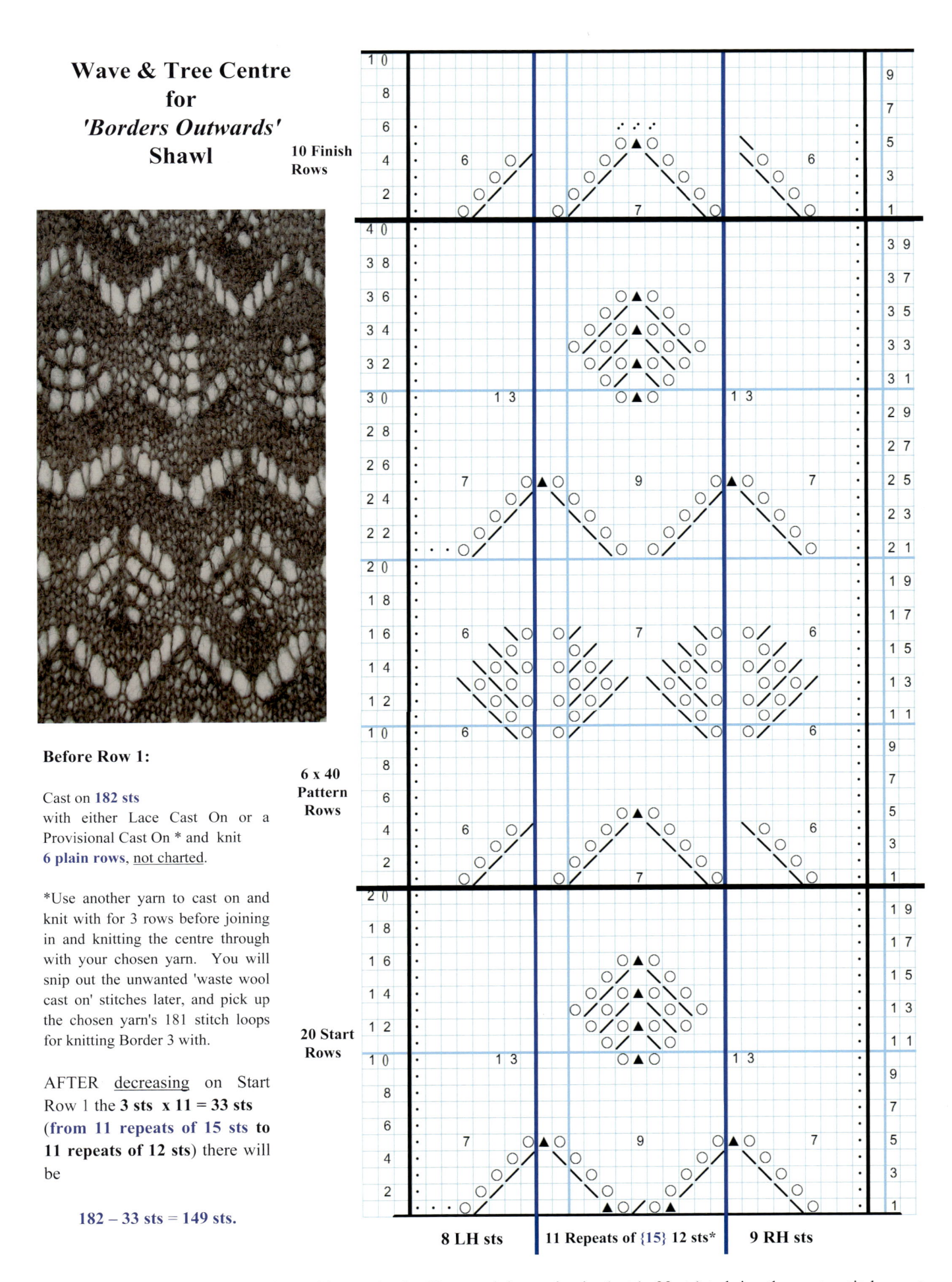

8 LH sts | **11 Repeats of {15} 12 sts*** | **9 RH sts**

Before Row 1:

Cast on **182 sts** with either Lace Cast On or a Provisional Cast On * and knit **6 plain rows**, not charted.

*Use another yarn to cast on and knit with for 3 rows before joining in and knitting the centre through with your chosen yarn. You will snip out the unwanted 'waste wool cast on' stitches later, and pick up the chosen yarn's 181 stitch loops for knitting Border 3 with.

AFTER decreasing on Start Row 1 the **3 sts x 11 = 33 sts** (**from 11 repeats of 15 sts to 11 repeats of 12 sts**) there will be

182 − 33 sts = 149 sts.

At Finish Rows 5 & 6, there is mirrored <u>increasing</u> by 33 sts and <u>decreasing</u> by 1 st (= 32 sts) to bring the centre stitch count back up to 149 + 32 = **181 sts.**

Total of 276 rows : 6 plain + 20 Start rows + (6 x 40 Pattern rows = 240) + 10 Finish rows.

*The 'Number of Stitches per repeat' changes down with Start Row 1 and up again with Finish Rows 5 - 6 as described above - this telescoping can't be shown on a chart.

Grey 2 Ply Lerwick Lace Shawl *Borders Outwards* Method : Chart 1 Rows 1 - 55

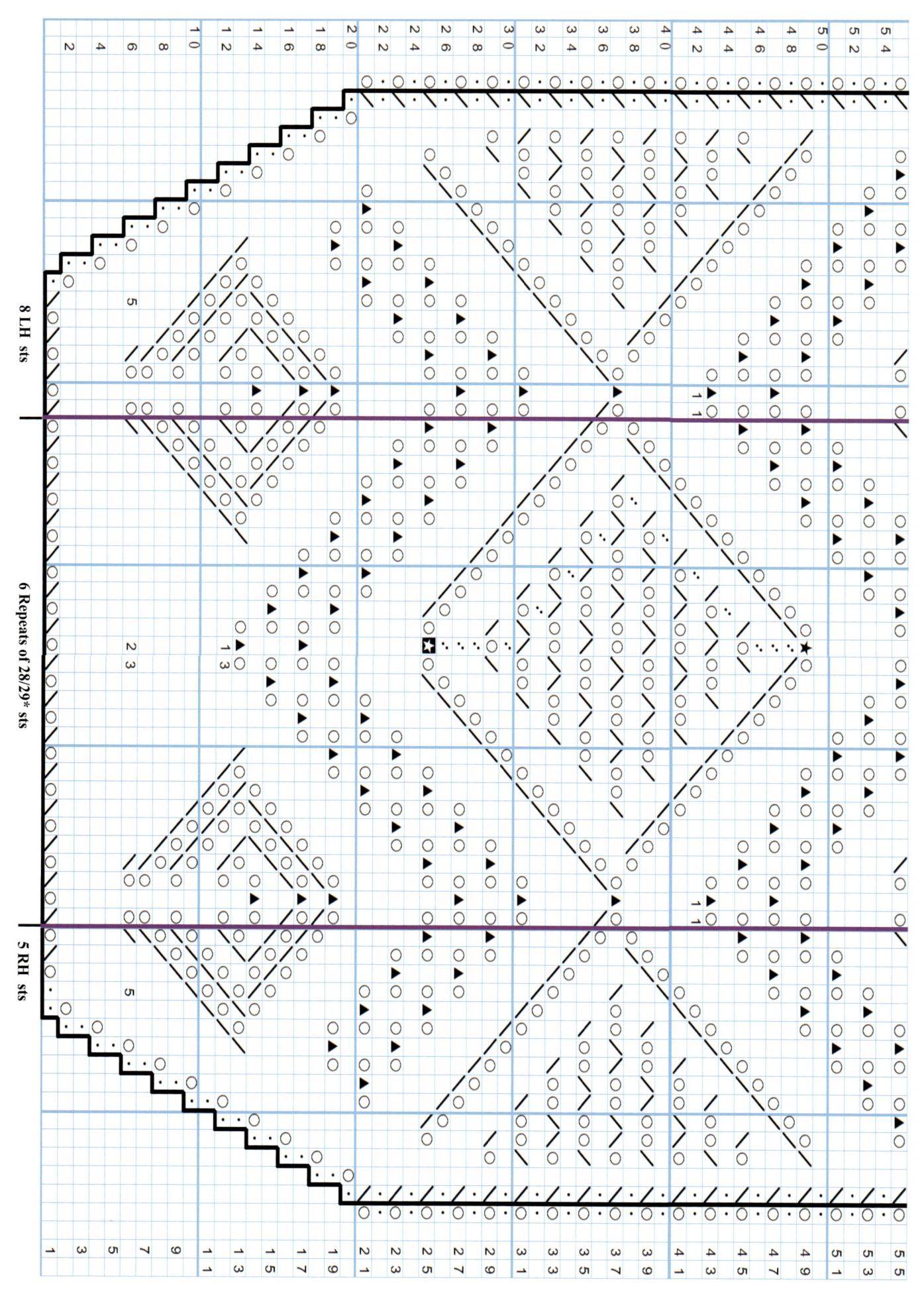

* = The Lacehole motifs with '\OO/' in them are even number based, so an extra stitch has to be made for them to be neatly centred in between the plain stitches of the diamonds. Knit into front and purl into the back of each 'OO' on the following rows. See page 17.

Grey 2 Ply Lerwick Lace Shawl *Borders Outwards* **Method – Chart 2 Rows 56 - 108**

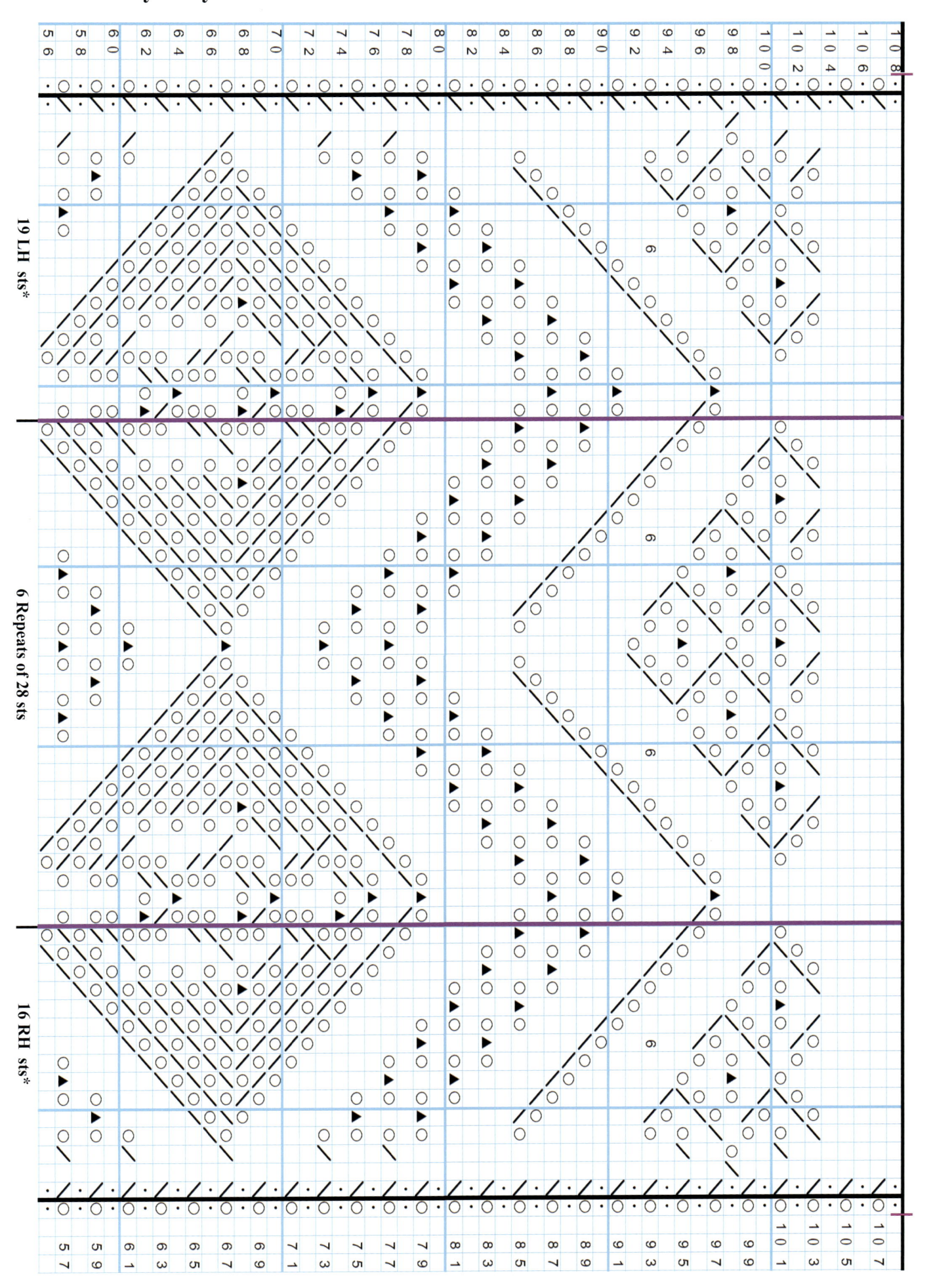

* = Not counting the 'O' sts outside black chart lines that define the sides from Row 21. Row 108 : **19 LH sts** + (6 x 28 sts = 168) + **16 RH sts** = **203 sts** for each border = **29** edging points. Increase approx every 10th st on final row to **224 sts** if you want **32** edging points.

Lerwick Lace Shawl
Mitred
Borders Outwards

Chart Rows 21 – 108
Continued on
Rows 1 – 20, page 26.
See notes on that page and
Overview page 13.

* = ' + 1 extra stitch' per motif for Rows 24 - 47

Note The long pink bar lines that show stitch Repeats (|) are moved from the points on page 26. Please move any markers in your knitting to match new positions.

Rows 105 - 108:
(9 x 28 sts = 252) + 11 side sts
= **263 sts**. Knit 3 plain rows,
increase to **266 sts**.
Work **38 edging points** per border:
(38 x 7 = 266), see page 9.

5 LH sts

9th Repeat

7 Repeats of 28* sts – as inset

8th Repeat

6 RH sts

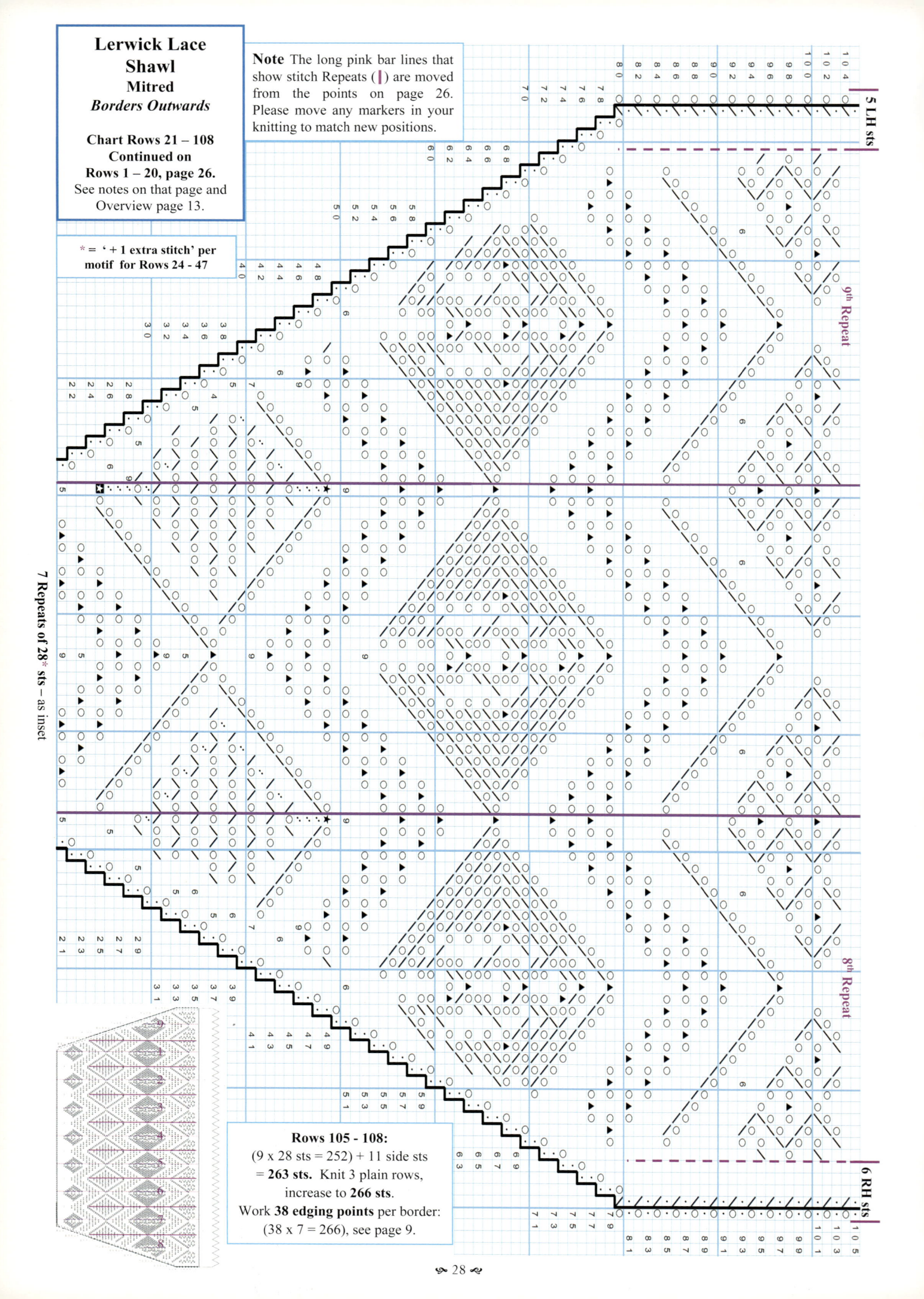

~ 28 ~

Appendix 1 : 'Running and Rooing'

Modern breeding since the 1900s and more particularly from the 1940s, has led in many ways to a different class of animal to those shown in the following early 20th century pictures, and clipping has almost completely replaced rooing since the 1960s. This all means the wool used in antique Shetland shawls differs from what we can use today – not only are the animals not the same, but neither is the widespread practice of the necessary skills of which rooing and hand-spinning were but two of the essentials in the making of ultra-fine gossamer plied lace yarn (see Eliza Edmonston's description, page 37).

But despite these many and frequently necessary changes, I will hand-on-heart totally endorse modern Shetland wool for traditional Shetland lace. In my experience it still retains the highly regarded drape and warm "soft handle" qualities not revealed till after the first dressing, so still continues to make a perfect marriage of yarn to pattern and tradition. The following extracts and images record something of how antique Shetland wool for this unique lace first came about.

In Shetland the free-roaming sheep were walled <u>out</u> of tiny fields called *'plantie crubs'*. Here, four such tiny fields are up the 'Burn of Hoswick' in a line, a crofter is bent tending the most distant one in about c1910. Other methods aimed at confining sheep include wired fences : a long one crosses the background of the postcard image above. Below, nimble footed sheep forage on a cliff; Shetland sheep were particularly keen to eat seaweed at certain times of the year.

The Observer June 1930 "Evacuation of St Kilda" :

"……**the St Kildan sheep are practically wild animals. They have run free and unhampered on their rocky island for a long period. They have never been sheared. The shepherds, with sheep dogs, who are now endeavouring to round them up, are having a difficult time. The sheep, unused to human beings and dogs, bite the dogs that are herding them……. The only practical method with most of the sheep is to throw them over the cliffs and pick them up out of the sea."**

Michael Powell, the influential and charismatic British film director of 1930s was charmed by the above newspaper clipping about the deliberate depopulation of an isolated Hebridean island off the west of Scotland. Looking for a suitable location for a telling of a similar tale (he was denied St Kilda itself), he became enchanted by what he saw as a comparably disappearing Shetland way of life – on the other side of Scotland. To record that before it too, vanished, he filmed a "voluntary evacuation" based around a simple love story as *The Edge of the World*, 1936, which he set on Foula; an isolated rocky Shetland island that still has a tiny population today, arguably as a direct result of that film. He also wrote a delightful vivid book memorialising his experiences *200,000 ft : The Edge of the World*, E P Dutton & Co Inc. 1938. (The Preface explains the '200,000 ft' relates to the footage filmed - edited to 7,000 ft). There, Powell describes the time honoured rooing that he filmed on Foula in 1936, a practice that must date from earliest farming days. He records that dogs weren't used to round up sheep on Foula as the animals were too wild (he had now learnt that the actual St Kildan practice was to use dogs to 'down' individual sheep by grasping their wool with filed teeth). So, in August on Foula he writes, there is The Run, the 'sheep runnings' in which elderly men, youngsters, men not engaged in the fishing, and women take due part. In small, pre-assigned groups they feign an aimless sauntering nearer and nearer the sheep who watch this pretence with deep suspicion :

" **but the sheep know better. Sooner or later they are spotted by some cynical-eyed matron, whose mass of dragging tangled wool, half on, half off her back and shoulders, gives her a horrible similarity to the leering semi-undress of a mid-Victorian brothel and show that she has avoided 'rooing' for two seasons and will be got into a krö only over your dead body……….**

A Foula sheep's one object in life is to avoid being run and rooed and to achieve it they will scramble, double and dodge……they short-cut down the cliffs like chamois, are as cynical as goats and as clever as monkeys……….others stop dead and lie down, preferring to be charged over rather than rooed." (pages 230, etc.)

After much effort in which the fine military tactic of "cutting off all retreat" is utilised, almost all the sheep are finally contained in secretly built *'krös'* - the sites of these had to be frequently changed as the Foula sheep 'know a thing or two' and get wise to their locations after a couple of rooings in the same place. Then, the older women and men - and all available hands indeed, grab each 100 pound weight of adult sheep one after the other, and start rooing : **"the short, fine wool is pulled off in quick handfuls, the overcoat separating for the undercoat like the husk of a ripe walnut."** Michael Powell says the whole process took about 10 minutes per sheep (yielding on an average, 2lbs / 900g of wool) before it is allowed to bounce "indignantly" away with an even more bitter determination not to be run and rooed next year.

There isn't any actual footage of lace knitting, but the film - now on DVD - is deeply evocative, and does in passing, record the women folk habitually knitting (mainly haps) along with many mystically beautiful and atmospheric scenes of crofting in an unbounded landscape; a way of life at the point of change to the modern. Powell's story concludes with the happy reunion of the young couple and the sad abandonment of their native fictional 'Hirta' for life on the Mainland, where there'll be readier access to necessities such as peat (for fuel, the isles are virtually tree-less. In the story, Hirta's peat deposits were about exhausted); doctors, work, etc. Knitters interested in Shetland will find this worth watching not only for a good story well told, but also for the reasonably accurate description of life in Foula in the 1930s that Powell was so keen to capture. A rare, perhaps unique, portrayal of a Shetland way of life that had continued almost unchanged in substance for decades.

SHEEP ROOING, SHETLAND — C. J. WILLIAMSON, SCALLOWAY

The postcard image above was taken c1930s and I believe shows the transition from traditional hand *'rooing'* – plucking naturally shed wool locks from a sheep's fleece, and modern hand shearing : the man on the right appears to be using hand clippers. Rooing was done on the ground as the semi-wild animals were restrained and then wool could be plucked in handfuls.

As described earlier, all available men and women took part in the summer *'caain'* (corralling of sheep into enclosures *'punds'* or *'krös'*, *'croos'*) and the annual collection of wool, usually in June. The semi-wild sheep were the only unwilling participants, often performing startling athletic feats to outwit capture, not from any real fear of pain but because this temporary confinement interfered with their free roaming habits. Many chose to leap down cliffs and were then the reluctant subjects of "rescue", each had to be slung one at a time across a man's shoulders as he climbed the cliff. Really *'fialskit'* (SM : also recorded as *'filsket'*, meaning frisky) or struggle-some sheep were hobbled as above left for rooing - the plucker's knee resting on the animal's neck whilst two or three of the sheep's legs were tied together; other folk helping with pacifying and restraining. More simply, one person held the animal calm whilst another plucked; and more unusually, one person could roo some animals unaided. As shown above, clipping had the advantage of being able to be done by one person more often; a factor which in time outweighed the cost of loss of length to the 'staple' or 'locks' - length of wool. Naturally shed neck locks could commonly be as much as in the region of 8 – 9* inches, or even up to double that (Dr Anderson 1790). As perhaps can be seen above, a uniformly shorn fleece would adversely affect this lock length – again, perhaps by as much as a quarter - as well as exposing the sheep to the cold more, as is mentioned in the extract *The Knitters* by Eliza Edmonston in the Appendices. Howsoever, the longer, finer locks, the *'haslock'* from the throat (*'hass'*), neck and shoulders, were always the best quality and often specially saved at the time of rooing for later hand-spinning into the gossamer lace yarn for shawls and veils. Shearing a fleece off 'all-in-one' would mean an extra sorting job later to retrieve this premium wool before it was parcelled into qualities for ordinary lace, mill spinning, for cloth, etc.

*"Improving" Shetland sheep by cross-breeding with other sheep (such as Merino AKA 'Spanish'; Cheviot and Blackface) has been on record since 1780 and most probably took place before that; so what 'true' Shetland sheep characteristics were like in ancient days is a subject of ongoing research / debate: Obviously it depends on which 'flock animal' was studied where, and at what date. It is recorded though that in contrast to the huge numbers of free-running sheep there were on Shetland certain native *'Kindly'* sheep which, in the 1800s were not left to run wild but were folded near the croft, and closer guarded; as their much softer wool was especially valued. DNA testing of antique exhibits should throw more light in time on precise qualities (such as lock length) and also on the mixed genetic stock that made and makes the Shetland sheep.

A Shetland ewe, c 1930 scrutinises the photographer for his intentions. Her wool has been rooed recently and we can better see her body's lean lines. Note the longer length of the new 'naturally tipped' coat exposed by rooing.

SHETLAND EWE

Appendix 2 : *Extracts from Frank Barnard's Picturesque Life in Shetland* George Waterston 1890

(SM: Dates are 1828 – 1895. The plates of 1889 for this lovely insightful book are in watercolours. Not much is yet recorded of this artist, he may be Michael Faraday's nephew on his wife's side - an art-student in Paris that Faraday writes to in 1852. The 1891 census records him as 63, single, a "Writer, Colour Painter, Sculptor", living at 320 Liverpool Road, London; this address he gives in the book's Preface. It is his unmarried sister's house, where he lives together with another unmarried sister - both Jane and Kate live on their 'own means'; there's also a brother Alfred 48, who is a Silversmith's clerk; and a servant Ada, 31.)

" **PLATE XXI. SHAWL-DRESSING.**

In a work like this, aiming at introducing Shetland and its people to the artistic and travelling public, it would be an unpardonable omission to pass by its hosiery in silence. The importance of this as a Shetland industry, ministering first of all to the comfort of the people simply as clothing, and next to their elegance of attire, especially among the women, cannot fail to be recognised on the most superficial glance at the islands.

The present excellence of Shetland woollen manufactures may be traced to the following causes among others : the possession of a rare quality of wool in the native sheep, the exigencies of climate impelling the people to produce for themselves suitable modes of attire, and, lastly, the presence of natural dyes in abundance. The more substantial articles of clothing — socks, comforters, caps, haps, &c. — were in existence and common use long before what is now called "Shetland hosiery" saw the light of day ; for while warm knitted garments date back for centuries, the tasteful and delicate fabrics now seen in ladies' shawls, veils, drawing-room curtains, neckties, &c., were first produced about fifty years ago. Cowie says :

" **In olden times the hosiery goods chiefly for exportation consisted almost exclusively of coarse stockings, gloves, and nightcaps, in which a large trade was done every summer during the palmy days of the Dutch herring fishery......Nor have the close-knitted goods of the Zetland women always been of coarse texture, ladies' stockings having been frequently produced of so fine a thread that a pair could be drawn through a lady's finger-ring. In former times various native dyes were used; they are still employed, but have to a great extent been superseded by indigo and cochineal. The variegated and fantastic hues which characterise such articles as the Fair Isle hosiery, and the more common bedquilts and hearthrugs are obtained from native dyes, chiefly lichens**." Thus, reddish purple, blackish purple, yellowish brown, and orange are derived from lichens while black is produced from peat-moss impregnated with bog iron-ore. While on the subject of dyes, it should be mentioned that the native chromates, particularly those of Unst, form a considerable part of the dye material which the Shetlander finds to his hand. One of the best colours seen in Shetland knitted goods, a dark grey-brown, is from the natural called by the people " murid," or " moorat," which is the modern form of the old Norse word " moor-red ."

The beauty of the well-known Shetland shawls is in the minds of most persons associated chiefly with some fashionable shop in the genteeler quarters of London and Edinburgh ; and it may raise a fresh interest to view these tasty items of feminine attire as adding a grace all their own to the stern features of a Shetland landscape — not, indeed, by covering the shoulders of the fair travellers exploring these regions, but as I have attempted to depict them, decking the rocky lea, like, gigantic spiders' webs, and doing their part, with dock, buttercup, and ragwort, in softening the rugged lines of the granite strata which stand out from the thin soil in many parts. This is an effect of the operation called shawl-dressing. Let us suppose that rain has fallen in torrents for a week past; many hours, or even days, of assiduous work in spinning, knitting and stitching, occupying the inmates of a group of cottages within doors, have produced a number of finished fabrics, dainty white lacy shawls, with the usual Zigzag stripe, double or treble, the stripe a delicate pink, blue, or dove grey on a field of white ; or coarser shawls, with black zigzags divided by thin white lines of mouse colour, iron grey, or dark brown. But now a fine breezy morning shines upon the Shetland lea, a brisk, drying nor'-wester brushes over grass and heather. The housewives sally forth with basketsful of soft, white knitting, damp from the wash, and each proceeds to peg down her shawls upon the grass where it is short, and free from the larger meadow plants, as dock, nettles, &c. Each shawl requires from forty to fifty pegs; extended on these, at a height of six inches above the soil, the wind passing freely above, below, and through its many interstices, it strains tighter and tighter as it dries. Every hour the judicious worker, peg-basket in hand, revisits the scene, relaxing or tightening as she readjusts the pegs, till every strong but delicate thread has stiffened into the proper degree of tension, in that geometrical regularity which characterises the whole work. Several hours thus pass till the shawl is properly dressed; it is then methodically folded up and put away, and when brought out for sale or exportation, it is fit for the bosom and neck of a duchess.

Edmonstone, speaking of Shetland hosiery, says : "**At the beginning of this century £17,000 worth of stockings were exported in one year. In 1840 fine Shetland shawls were first sent to market, followed by veils and neckties.**" *(SM: scarves.)* Tudor tells us : "**The finest Shetland wool which is very scarce, and every year becoming scarcer, is reserved for the very finest shawls and veils. Each district has its own speciality in the hosiery line. Thus Northmaven produces soft underclothing; Nesting, stockings; Walls and Sandsting, socks and haps (shoulder shawls); Whiteness and Weesdale** (sic)**, fancy coloured gloves; Lerwick, shawls and veils.** "

Shetland shawls, pretty as they are, nearly all bear the stamp of a certain primitiveness. The cultured design which marks the textile fabrics of France might be studied, with advantage by Shetland knitters, who, having begun on a few good patterns, supplied to them probably many years ago, continue too much by rule of thumb. This industry in its present form dates from about 1830, when Mr E. Standen of Oxford introduced new styles of patterns and developed the industry. The cheapness of these pretty articles is one of their great recommendations; they can be washed, re-dressed, mended again and again, and need only the beautifying influence to take an honourable place among the textile manufactures of our country. "

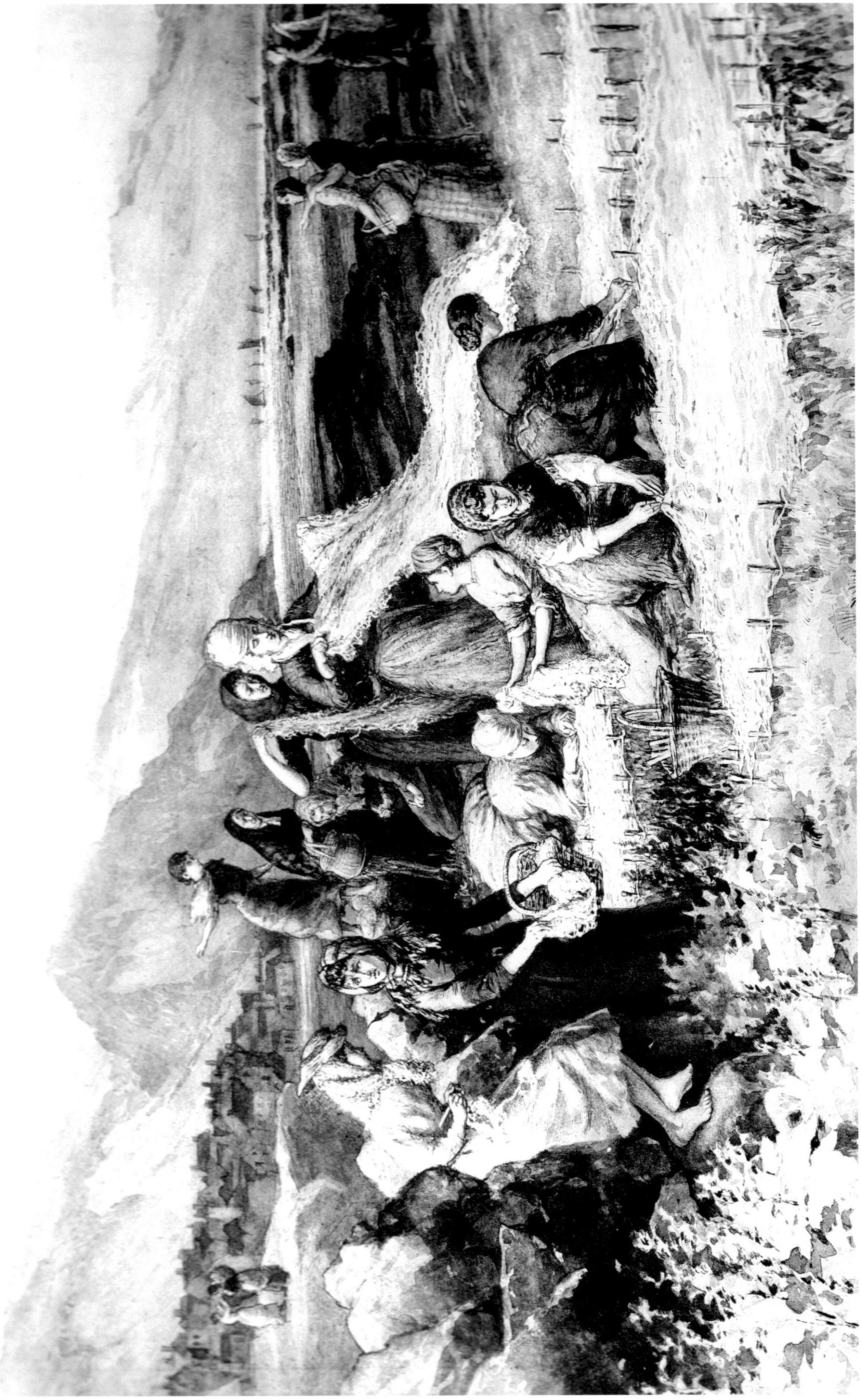

Additional knitting-related plates from Frank Barnard's *Picturesque Life in Shetland*, which was a book of only 300 copies :

A Shetland Grandmother has that invaluable family member shown minding the baby while spinning; mother is putting up fish to dry whilst "auntie", a herring worker by day, is choosing from her **"store of shawls, haps and mufflers and caps"** for an evening's **"junketing"** (*SM: visiting*) : **"the shawls are mainly the work of her own busy fingers, for which her mother is spinning the wool, which was on the sheep's back a few days ago."**

Next page :
Stepping Stones shows Shetlanders out *'treavellling'* – journeying, the spinning wheel *'spinnie'* going with them; women with shoulder shawls tied around laden baskets, their clothing is elsewhere described :

"The costume of the women is of course a notable feature. In the older ones deep-toned shawls, green, plaid, or black, envelop shoulder and head ; from beneath these juts the snow-white cap frill ....*(SM: with its chequered ribbon or "haap" tied over it under the chin)***......seeming originally designed to protect the ears from keen wind. In the younger women the turban-like folds of the headkerchief, green, white, yellow, or striped variously, or, better still, their bossy** (*SM: meaning 'thickly textured'*) **plaits of dark shiny hair, with shoulder shawls of many degrees of fineness and bright striped petticoats, give a rich vivacity to the peopled scene...............which reminded .... [one] ...of Venice......"** (Extract of text to *The Market Boat*).

and *Those Women's Tongues* which, in my opinion, illustrates a rather acidic masculine view* of women who are :

"fascinated by the gossip of the village, the price of lambs in Lerwick, the quality of the late Bressay potatoes, the bonnet ribbons, head-shawl, and lace flounces of Miss K-, the scarlet petticoat of Mrs X-" ....
"All Shetland women can talk as they knit ; all Shetland women can knit as they walk ; but carding and spinning requires the sitting posture, and this again greatly favours talking. The two operations go on at all seasons, but the long winter evenings are specially the time when women and girls congregate around or near the peat fire for this sort of work......Well, the lamp lights up as best it may the evening scene – either the pair of gossips, the trio or ring of women ; for neighbours have free access to each others houses at all times. Two or three spinning wheels of various shape and pattern, the old-fashioned tripod with three straddling legs, and the commoner long-shaped form with its treadle, pirn, and reels appear as needful adjuncts. Every woman not busied in spinning takes her "cards" and places her heap of wool, white, brown, or grey, down by her right foot, from which the cards are continuously supplied. The wool, which up to this time by its short wreathy curls reminds one of the nimble black and white faced little quadrupeds which run or skip from heathery knoll to knoll, is now teased out by the wiry combs till it shines soft and glistening as thistledown and so passes on to the spinner."

*Remember, he's a lifelong bachelor at this date (and probably remains so till his death only a few years later), living with two spinster sisters. Look at the mournful expression he gives the "out of it" "veteran" in the picture!

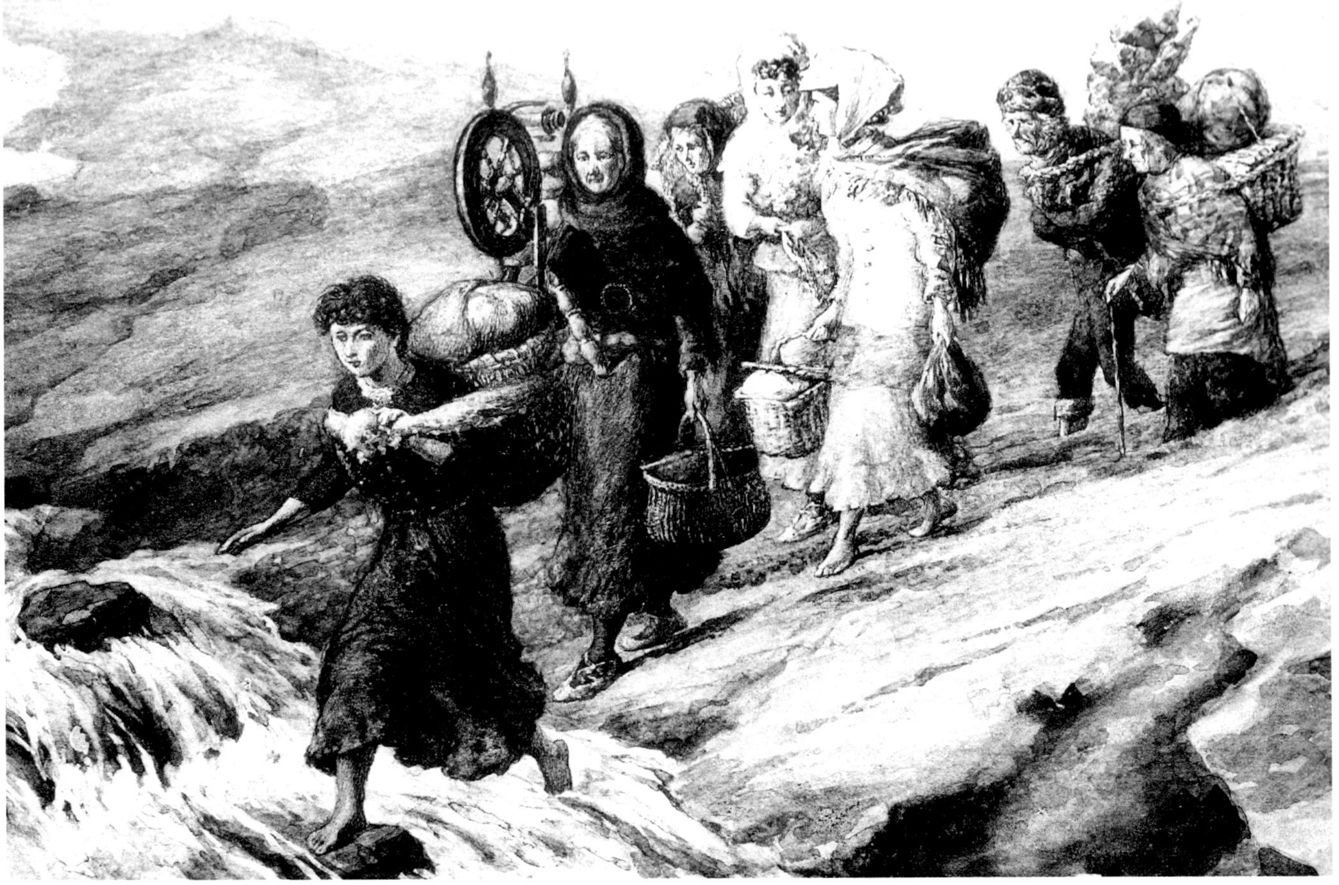

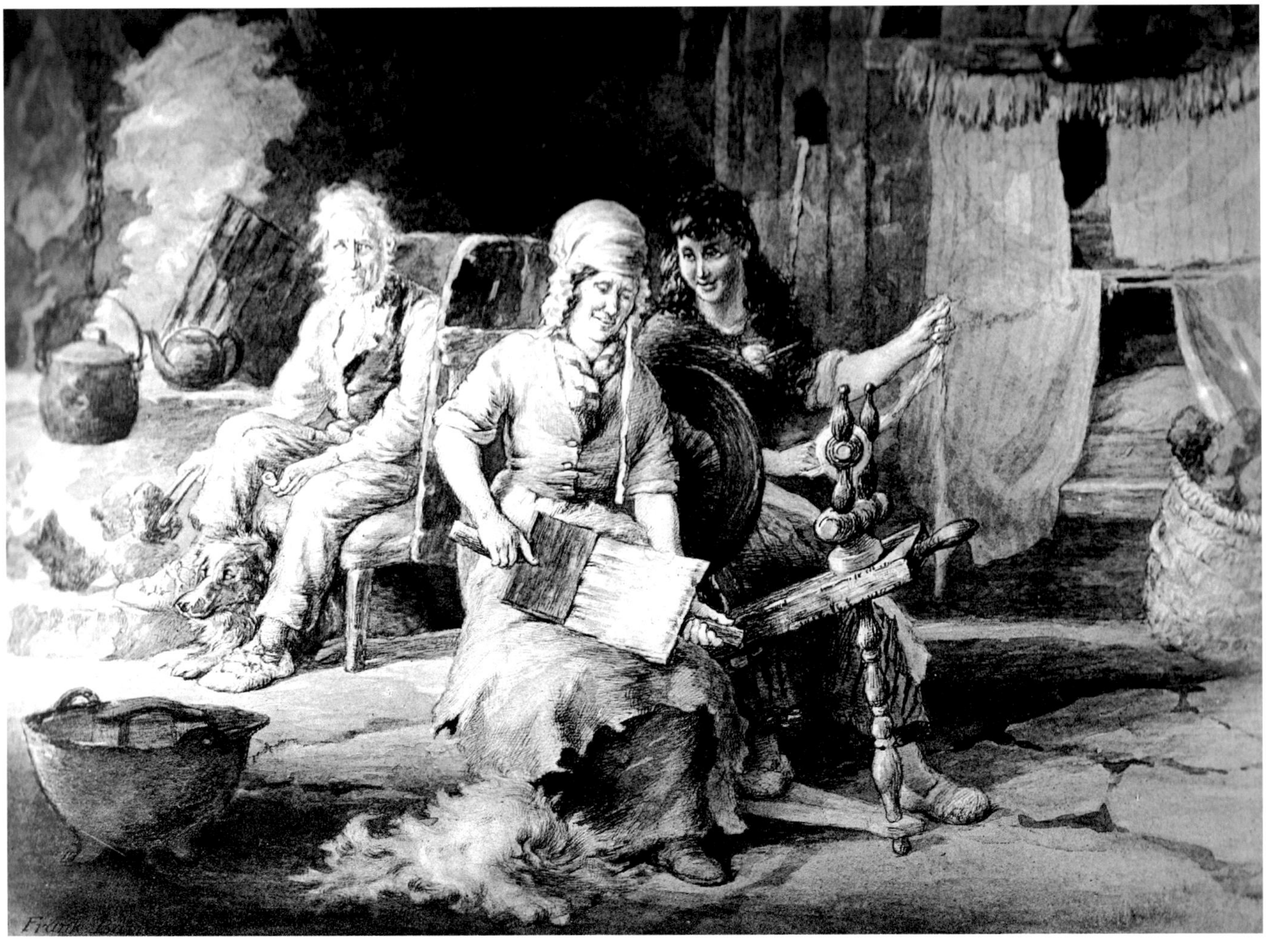

Appendix 3 : "The Knitters" *from*

SKETCHES AND TALES OF SHETLAND 1856. By **Eliza (Tod MacBriar) Edmonston, 1801-1869.**

(SM: This fascinating woman married Laurence Edmonston MD of Unst, in Dublin 1824. Eliza was a promoter of Shetland knitting and a keen knitter herself - she developed a technique of 'tapestry knitting' rugs in reversible colours – see Scottish Knitting, Helen Bennett, Shire, page 29, where there is a rare photograph of her with her rugs, which feature large geometrically patterned squared designs.

Jessie Saxby was her daughter, one of eleven children. A Shetland folklorist born 1842, Jessie lived to be over 90 years old; James Norbury says Jessie too in turn, also encouraged the development of local knitted lace patterns by showing her own lace collection to Shetland knitters, though there is a small possibility he may have meant a 'Jessie Scanlon'- see History of Knitting, Richard Rutt.)

FISH being the most valuable commodity of the Shetland Islands, and its produce and preparation for the market being the chief ostensible dependence of the people, the cares of the house, and labour on the little farms, are left in a great measure to the females. Only in seed-time and harvest, do the men, as a general rule, give anything like steady assistance in the working of the land. The industry of the men then is but desultory. Because of the uncertainty of the weather, they will remain many days at their lodges, waiting, and doing nothing while they wait, for the favourable moment to put off to sea. It were greatly to be desired, that they would employ these unfilled-up hours with some light and handy occupation, - knitting for example, which appears to be every way suitable ; but unfortunately they consider it so scornfully effeminate, that we have heard of only one or two men who are good knitters; and they are ashamed to avow it, and practise it only in secret; and yet the Highland, Irish, and Faroe men, make considerable sums by the knitting of coarse hose and seamen's frocks.

The Shetland females, on the other hand, are constantly and energetically industrious, - not only in hoeing potatoes, making hay, and drying and grinding corn, but in such heavy work, as carrying sea-weed for manure, - digging the ground with the spade, and harrowing in the seed. And then, every moment that is not occupied in these and other necessary operations of the household and farm, is filled up with knitting. You will never see a Shetland woman without work of this kind in her hand, - whether with her keyshie of peats on her back, or seated on the sober pony, with which she goes often several miles to bring home dried moor-grass for fodder, or fish from the seaside, - whether talking to you, or paying or receiving a visit, - all the while she plies swiftly the knitting-pins or wires. The younger women, whose sight is still good, and whose fingers are supple, have always two pieces of worsted work in progress at a time, - the brown wool stocking for odd moments, or in the twilight, or when going about, - and the fine lace-like shawl or veil, for the long evenings, or half holiday in which the daughters of a family indulge themselves in turn. Socks for home use, or for sale, are always the work of the old women.

There being no sort of manufactories, or openings for the regular industry of the females, excepting only knitting, they have happily so applied themselves to this art, as to have brought it to great perfection, and secured for it a pretty regular demand, to which also the peculiar softness and fineness of the native wool, no doubt in a considerable measure contributes.

The sheep of Shetland are of a peculiar breed, indigenous to the country. They are very small, and, of course, wild and hardy. Strangers, indeed, who see these little, odd-looking creatures, shy as deer, scampering along at a speed almost as great, can hardly be persuaded they are of the sheep genus at all.

The liberty of pasturage on the uninclosed commons, *(SM: unwalled, unfenced off moorland shared by the inhabitants)* is included in the holding of the fisherman's small farm. The people, therefore, keep as many animals as they can, and the pastures consequently are always overstocked.

Most of the cottars have a few sheep, and some more fortunate or more careful than their neighbours, have stocks of from twenty to a hundred, which are all marked in a peculiar manner in the ears, each family retaining through generations its own mark. They are never folded or fed, but at certain intervals, are driven by dogs, and a multitude of owners, to small ponds (or *croos),* for the purpose of being counted, marked, rooed, or occasionally taken for sale or slaughter. Comparatively few are doomed to the fate last mentioned, as the animals are chiefly valued for their wool; but severe seasons, and other casualties, to which the more than half-wild creatures are subject, prevent them from increasing, as they might do, under a better regulated system. The ewes hardly ever have more than one lamb at a birth, and, in consequence of sufficient males not being reserved, the females often do not bring forth at all. Moreover, worrying dogs and sheep-stealing *bipeds (SM: er, thieves!)* commit great depredations on the flocks with absolute impunity. It might, one should think, be easily so managed by the proprietors of the soil, that no tenant should have above a stipulated number of sheep on the common, - that a proper proportion of rams should be retained, - and that some local supervision should be appointed for the prevention of *robbery* and *murder.* The cottagers being for the most part tenants at will, the landlords possess great power over them, which in days gone by, they have been accused of discreditably abusing. It would seem, they have *now* run to the opposite extreme of indulgence, and too much neglect to exercise, in a wholesome enlightened manner, the influence which their situation gives them. Passing strange indeed it appears that most of the Shetland lairds are so blind to their own interest, in which, of course, that of their dependents are involved, as to neglect all regulation and oversight in the breeding both of sheep and of ponies. On the former, a large proportion of the people's resources depends; and the latter, now almost equally disregarded, might be made even more productive of valuable returns.

The Shetland sheep are of various colours, besides black and white. They are of almost every shade of brown and grey, and some are piebald. The wool is also of very different quality, even on the same animal, the finest being about the throat and back. Nevertheless even the coarser portions have a velvety softness, quite peculiar. Several causes have been assigned for this distinguishing property, besides the exclusiveness of the breed. One is the scant but often highly aromatic pasture of the Shetland hills, and another, that the wool is never shorn, but *rooed,* that is, pulled with the fingers from the creature's back, lock by lock. It must be remembered, that sheep, like many other animals, yearly change their coating. Hence, as the season advances the wool becomes loose; the animal then rubs it along the heather, which acts as a comb ; and, indeed, a fair wool harvest is often gained in this way by the poorer ownerless persons *(SM: I believe she means people who don't own any sheep)*, who gather what is left among the stones and heath. At the time then, when the fleece becomes loose, which is in June, about a month after lambing time, the sheep are collected, and their wool pluckd off by women, who are sufficiently tender in the operation, so that the rooing gives no pain, but is rather relief to the animal. There is, moreover, left on the skin, a considerable quantity of long hair, provided by nature for several species of animals in northern latitudes to protect them more completely from the inclemency of the weather, and this, it is obvious, would be totally removed were shears employed on the sheep.

The wool being brought home, is carefully separated into its different colours and qualities. There is nothing of which the Shetland housewife is so proud, or takes so much care, as her stock of wool. The coarsest is set aside for the fisherman's socks and mittens ; a second quality is used for a sort of twilled blanketing, woven by some superannuated fishermen, in a very primitive handloom. This *claith* (so it is called), if grey or mixed, is dyed with indigo, and makes very durable jackets and trousers ; if white, it is used for blankets and petticoats, or under-shirts for the men. The brown wool is almost entirely made into ladies' stockings, and the best of the grey into gentlemen's socks, of which a few pairs will always be found, on inquiry, in every cottage, awaiting an opportunity of sale. If none else offers, these hose are bartered at the shops for cotton goods, or any other sort of clothing the seller may require ; and, in general, it is understood, in this system of exchange, that the merchants require considerable profits to secure themselves against risks, and to allow for freights, &c. A greater loss arises to the poor cottars, from travelling pedlars, who tempt them with worthless trumpery, and carry off the produce of their industry at very low prices.

The spinning is all done by hand on a common lint-wheel *(SM: a wheel originally designed for spinning linen)*. The staple of the wool is very short, and it is said, cannot, on that account, be so well managed by machinery. The same circumstance accounts also for the fact, that Shetland hose, however pleasant in wear, are not very durable.

The finest wool is not carded, but combed out, and then teased by the fingers. It is mixed with grease, or a little fine oil, and a few persons who are very expert can spin, from two ounces of raw wool, *six thousand yards* of three-ply thread, - a sufficient quantity to make a good sized shawl. This process is very tedious, and requires manipulation so nice, that very few persons ever attain the art in perfection. More usually a veil may be made of half an ounce, and a shawl of four or five ounces of wool. This will serve to explain, that unlike Berlin and other wools, which are sold by weight, and spun by machinery, the finer the thread of Shetland worsted, the more the labour; it is therefore disposed of by the 'cut' or number of threads.

Weaving and Winding a Shetland Claith Web   Ramsay's Series Shetland Studies

Weaving on a loom at Swinister, Ronas Voe in about 1906. The man weaves on the loom and his son Henry Jamieson, is working a pirm wheel: winding wool from ready-spun hanks onto bobbins ready for his father to weave. Weaving was normally a "men-only" trade in Shetland.

Shetland has been celebrated for beautifully fine plain knitting, for the last century at least, and produced gloves for ten shillings and sixpence, and stockings for two guineas a pair, knitted on wires as fine as a sewing needle *(SM: UK 22 – 24)*.

It is believed the Duke of Medina Sidonea, admiral of the Spanish Armada, and his followers, whose ship was wrecked on Fair Isle, and who afterwards wintered in Shetland, were the first that taught these islanders the art of knitting. *(SM: This then popularly held and promoted romantic theory is widely discounted today, but may contain a kernel of truth - as oral 'myths' frequently are found to do).* Certain it is, that the painted-like manufacture of the Fair Isle people at this day, is quite similar to what is made in the South of Spain. But the open work knitting now so attractive to the poor artists, as well as to the public, is an invention for which the Shetland females themselves deserve all the credit. From the simplest beginnings, led on and encouraged by some ladies as a pastime, it has progressed from one thing to another, till it has attained its present celebrity, without the aid either of pattern-book, or of other instruction, than the diligence and taste of the natives themselves.

We are, indeed, aware, that in Madeira, Germany, Malta, &c., very fine specimens of knitting in cotton and silk threads are produced ; but after making every possible enquiry, we cannot make out, that they were in advance of the Shetlanders in the invention of the art , - still less, that the latter, since the days of the shipwrecked admiral aforesaid, have ever received any foreign instruction whatever in knitting. In confirmation of this statement, should such be required, we may just mention, that the patterns and terms here used in knitting, have a nomenclature all their own.

A Shetland knitter cannot comprehend a pattern from a book, if one is shewn to her; and should you attempt a translation for her benefit, she will hardly have patience to follow it, - ten times more quickly than you can read it, move her fingers and her thread, and ere the design is half completed, she knows what is intended, and finishes, - probably improves upon it, without more assistance.

In seasons of ordinary mildness, when the men may get pretty regularly to sea, and the corn is not shaken by September gales 'ere it is ripe, and the potatoes do not fail, the Shetland cottars are, with common care, tolerably comfortable. They must work rather hard, it is true, yet certainly not harder than labourers elsewhere ; and they have the advantage of being removed from many fluctuations in trade and manufactures, which often tell so hard on the labouring classes in otherwise more favoured latitudes. They are, if the expression may be allowed, more completely in the hands of Providence, since soft favouring weather is nearly all they require for a state of prosperity. But the ordinary course of events shews, that this is not to be expected in the geographical position of the country. Summer mildew, and harvest gales, often damage the crops, while frequent squalls, or heavy seas, render the fishing season unproductive or disastrous. Under these circumstances the knitting is a resource, the importance of which may hardly on cursory view be estimated ; and we trust the British public will not soon lose their taste for the handiwork of the poor Shetland artists.

Numerous instances might be adduced of whole families being rescued from absolute want, and even the rent of many a widowed mother paid, by the industry of the females in knitting alone, especially since the introduction of the fancy articles, where there is so much room for taste and application.

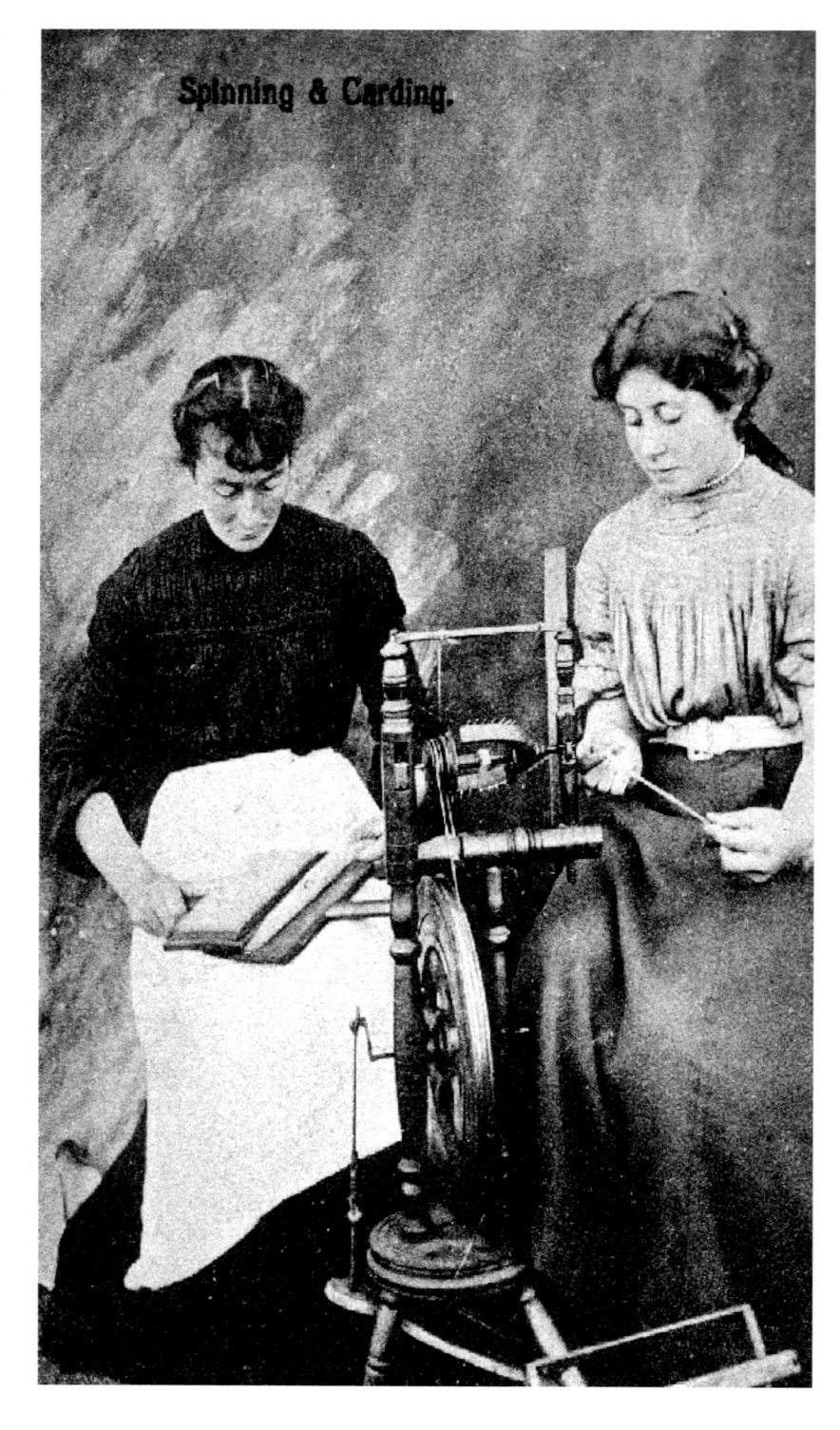

Spinning & Carding.

By the last census, the whole population in Shetland was deficient nearly a third in males. This arises in a great measure from the absence of the sailor part of the families, which, with the circumstance, that so many casualties befall the men at home, renders it quite common for whole households to be composed of only women and children. It may, indeed, be satisfactorily calculated, that three-fourths of the income of the Islands, if Lerwick be excluded, is assignable to the agency of the female sex. Let us sketch one little picture of Shetland life, that may perhaps illustrate some of these remarks.

One fine autumnal day, two strangers were returning from a pedestrian excursion to the western coast. Their feet were soaked with wet ; their hands begrimed ; their guns shouldered, and a fine water-spaniel trotted wearily at their heels. Thinking to make a short cut to their destined lodging for the night, they leaped a low fence of rough stones, topped with crumbling turf, and were crossing the little paddock it enclosed, when they perceived two females, seated on the grass, beside a small stack of peats, belonging to a cottage so low, it had been concealed from the strangers by a slight inequality of the ground. As they drew near, two girls rose respectfully to their feet, and the travellers stopped to ask their way. One of the girls seemed a little above twenty, of middle size, and gentle expression of countenance, and she was clad in tolerably tidy and deep mourning. The other was taller, but much more girlish in figure. Her dress consisted of a blue woollen petticoat, and a dark coloured jacket of cotton, over which was a 'kerchief of rusty black, and a broad band of the same sable hue tied down a coarse muslin cap. In her hand she held a half-finished sock she was knitting, over which she bent, turning at the same time half away, to conceal her face, for she was, and had been, weeping bitterly.

Of the strangers, we need only say, that one was young, heavily laden with multifarious trophies of his ramble, and looked like a student. His companion, who was the spokesman, was of middle size, and noble presence. Grounding their fowling pieces *(SM: guns)*, the travellers seated themselves on the turf-dyke, and the dog also gladly stretched himself for a rest, while a short colloquy took place. The lonely dwelling of which the girls seemed to be the inmates, was built on the common, a usual practice for the helpless females, who are not able to pay a farm rent ; because, if their friends will only raise for them the little cottage, they have nothing to pay for permission to occupy the site, and perchance *inclose* (*SM: enclose*) and break up *a few* roods of the thin barren soil, in which to plant some potatoes, with their peat ashes for manure. Annie, the elder sister, explained this to the stranger, who further asked of their parentage and employments ; and, by the kindliness of his eye, and the sympathy of his words and manner, he soon learnt their simple history. Their father had been lost at the *haff* (*SM: fishing*) long, long ago, — they did not remember him, — their mother had died a few days before and both the girls wept again. They had a brother, he was far away at sea, they knew not where, grief and anxiety respecting him had shortened their mother's life, and saddened her last hours. In the low hut, - the home of that mother's widowhood, there lived also an unmarried aunt, who attended to every thing; they loved her well, and she cherished them as her own. They had, moreover, a bed-ridden grandmother, who had a small pension from a merchant-seaman's fund, to which her deceased husband had subscribed, and this pittance of about two pounds a-year, was all the worldly dependence of this poor family, excepting what they earned by knitting. It was *a* most beautiful shawl that Annie held in her hands, nearly finished. "Aunty Mabel" knitted socks ; she could do a pair in a week, except when she was spinning ; their father's brother, who had a large family of his own, had given them a pet-lamb, which was now a "fine wooled" ewe, so that they had a little wool from her and her yearly lamb; sometimes they bought a little, and sometimes they worked in their neighbours' fields a few days for some more. Annie had been able, by the sale of some work, to purchase for herself decent mourning for her dear mother ; but Britta, the younger sister, had lately lived with her uncle, where she had to work so constantly on the farm, and in the dairy, she had no leisure for knitting ; she had not even learnt the open work patterns ; and she was now crying because " she could not go to the kirk, or any where, without right claes."

It may be observed here, that the Shetland peasants, both men and women, but especially the latter, never go abroad unless they are respectably clad. They have a decent pride in this, which is very creditable to them. Strangers often remark it, and because they witness not rags and squalor, are led to think the people are in better circumstances than is consistent with fact. But they do not see the shivering children, and crouching old people, - many of the latter kept *to bed* for lack of raiment ; or the borrowing from one another, even of those who are at church, and otherwise seen abroad; or the shame with which many a hard-working wife will hide herself even from her neighbours, that her girls may have the use of her best things. But to return to Annie and the kind looking stranger.

" Does not the uncle with whom she stays give your sister clothing as well as food? " asked he.

" Oh no," replied Annie, " even his own wife and daughters supply themselves with clothes by their handiwork. It's all the custom here, sir. "

" And why not *thus* your sister also? " demanded the gentleman.

She was silent. It was too evident the cousins took the time for their own knitting they denied to poor orphaned Britta. "And when or how is this probation to end ? " pursued the stranger. A slight respectful gesture shewed the cottage maiden did not understand the query.

" When does your sister expect she may procure what she wants?" explained he.

" Oh ! she will get a *har'st fee* in a while," Annie answered.
" She must then wait till after harvest ! - Is that shawl you are making for sale ? " " No, Sir. I got the yarn from a lady to knit it for her. " " But you will be paid for your work."

Two young peat workers, the girl knitting, the boy packing peats into his kishie c1910

" Oh, yes, sir ! but I owe something at the shop for my shoes. Aunty Mabel needs greatly some tea, and we have the casting of our peats to pay for yet."   *(SM: dried peat was the vital fuel in these treeless islands. 'Cast' peats are shown piled above).*

" You would help your sister if you could, would you not ? "

" Oh I blithely that sir," said Annie, while a more winning softness stole into her eye, " I have just been telling her that before har'st is come yet, I will have two or three veils made, and I will give her them to buy a black frock with."

" By-the-by," abruptly said the younger traveller, " have you a draught of milk you could let me have ?"

" We have no milk," responded Annie, " but some good *blaand* ; shall I get you some ?" " *Blaand* ! what may that be ?"

" The whey of churned milk sir," smiled Annie, it is the only drink we have, but it is very good, we get as much as we like from our neighbours who have *kye*. " *(SM: cows).*

" *Blaand* by all means then," said the strangers together, and Britta instantly stepped to the cottage, soon returning with a small bowl of whey. It proved sharply acidulous, and very refreshing to the weary and thirsty pedestrians.

" And now, have you not a pair or two of socks you could let me have," continued the elder stranger.

" Aunty has," promptly replied Annie, " But I fear only one pair finished; and again Britta was despatched to bring them.

The travellers then saw her face looking somewhat brighter. It was not beautiful, but the red pouting lips, and the long thick lashes shading soft eyes of bluish grey, made it look very sweet and interesting. The mass of crisply curling hair, was intended to stay under the close mourning cap, but one side during her weeping had fallen over her cheek dishevelled in wavy ringlets many a highbred beauty would have envied. Hastily pushing back the stray locks, and having dried her tears, she looked so charming that both the travellers gazed at her admiringly, while she presented the soft wool socks to the benevolent looking gentleman. Pulling out his purse, he put a piece of money into her hand, and the strangers went their way.

They had scarcely proceeded twenty yards when Britta exclaimed, " Annie ! it's gold, it's not a *shilling* ! " " Run after them, Britta," cried her sister. But Britta hung back from bashfulness and dread of strangers, whom she had hardly ever in her life before spoken to. Annie therefore hurried after the pedestrians, carrying the sovereign, and explained the mistake.

" Dear me !" exclaimed their kindly looking friend. " A sovereign ! — so it is, never mind, I cannot possibly take it back. Let your sister buy her mourning dress. Providence sent it her for that purpose, I suppose."

Annie was so surprised, she often afterwards thought, how strange it was, she had not even thanked the giver.

But needs it be told how Britta was cheered, - what a nice cup of tea, " granny" and "aunty" had that evening, - how Britta appeared at the kirk next Sunday, - and how, with more shrewdness than her gentler sister, she ever believed, the unknown had made no " mistake," but delicately intended the gracious and most acceptable present.

And, moreover, Britta stayed with her sister, instead of toiling hardly through a wet harvest for the fee not now needful. Thus she learnt thoroughly the finest knitting patterns, and very soon their joint work, with aunty Mabel's thrifty management, was sufficient to maintain them all in tolerable comfort, a consummation *(SM: here, an ending)* apparently very far off, had it not been for the stranger's well-timed gift.

THE END

Some Knitting Advice

Speak it quietly, but we all make mistakes and miscalculate – our shawl knitter did, but you'd need to do a thorough search to find her mistakes; and I can show you many exquisite lace pieces now in museums with glaring mistakes knitted in, but they aren't noticed by 99% of the visitors who just gasp deservedly, at the beauty of the work. Too many knitters get totally upset over the knowledge that there is a tiny error in the piece they are making and end up unravelling whole projects because of slightly less-than-perfect knitting. Don't stress please, to that extent – you'll ruin your enjoyment and peace of mind if you let tiny things get to you such as a 'mis-knit' no one else can see without you pointing it out. Just accept you will make mistakes, that doing so is part of learning, and then set about learning how to avoid or rectify them.

Many people are nervous about whether they are "up to doing a pattern" - that they'll get to a point in the border and stop, unclear of what to do next. If you aren't sure about a pattern and you've visually checked it through for whether you can do it or better, if you want to alter it more to suit your taste; it's a good idea to get into the habit of making samples – like mine on page 16, just cast on for 1 or 2 repeats and knit as charted (or as you've re-charted). This is a quick way to familiarise yourself with the pattern and so really saves mistakes later. You'll also find out what you really like - or don't, about a piece. Dress the sample and get a distance on it to see clearly what features please or irritate – I didn't like as much the pronounced line in the edging caused by using a double insertion; knowing this, I could change that before the shawl was made!

Regularly examine your knitting in progress – say every 10 or 20 rows – to look for serious mistakes such as dropped stitches, or 'misknitted' areas. It's <u>much</u> simpler to put right a mistake at an early stage, than to realise its presence when it's too late to correct.

Another very good habit is to learn the counting for each row – that there are always '7 plain stitches' between the pattern stitches for example. As you get to the '7th', just glance and check you're on course and about to do the pattern stitches as you should be: if not, have you dropped a stitch or missed an increase? You can easily pick up a previous row's dropped stitch, or knit into a strand if you've missed a 'make 1', or now put right a missed decrease. Oftentimes, a simple misknit can be put right by making/decreasing a stitch, but always check carefully the area beneath to ensure there isn't a rogue dropped stitch lurking to ladder (undo) later. As you get more expert, you'll be able to correct mistakes even several rows back in a pattern section, thereby avoiding the need to unravel.

Shetland lace knitting in progress always looks miserably shrivelled – as does all unshaped lace; so when checking, gently stretch each area of knitting over your knee as fully as you can and examine it. If you find a mistake, it might very well be easy to sort out - or, if the very worst has happened, you can undo that entire section of knitting. The " very worst" I'm visualizing here is a gaping, impossible-to-retrieve hole, a missed set of rows or a misplacing of a motif – something that will really disturb the entire harmony of design. These errors are best avoided by not doing complicated knitting such as "set up pattern Row 1"s of charts when tired or distracted, and by an automatic routine of checking of place in pattern chart and actual knitting. (Weave a length of coloured yarn around repeat groups of stitches when you 'set them up' on the first few rows - for this pattern, I'd suggest using it around the 'groups of 28' in the borders. This helps you locate the forming motifs.)

If it actually comes to it that you need to undo the last session of knitting and you're not confident that you can resume all the stitches, go over the area below it with spray starch and leave the knitting to dry. Then, when you do unravel the knitting, the stitches you don't want undone will be less likely to undo themselves - and the starch will wash out later. This

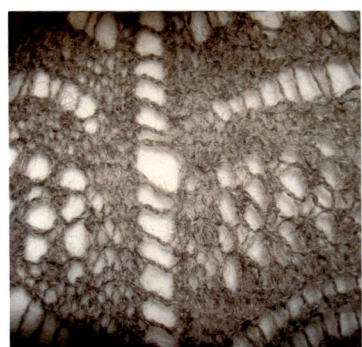

Here's two mistakes in my Grey shawl, one a mis-knitted increase in a 'seam' left; and one a mistake: a dropped stitch in a double decrease right, that came to light by "pinging open" as I dressed the shawl.

Many Shetland shawl dressers would be expert in small repairs, though it seems sometimes they'd miss one, see this exhibit of a 1930s fine shawl.
A good knitter should easily be able to repair this - it seems another decrease failed and so laddered here!

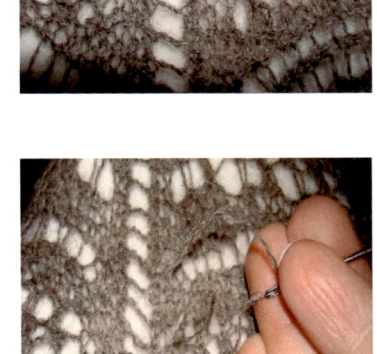

Needle and wool soon rectified both :

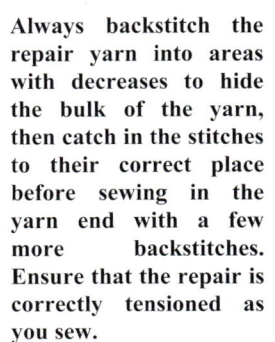

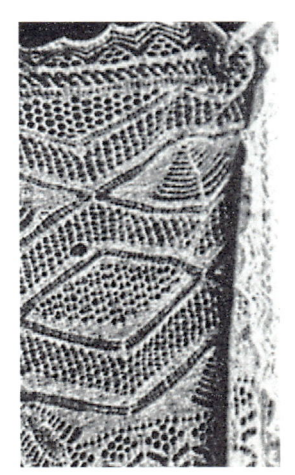

Always backstitch the repair yarn into areas with decreases to hide the bulk of the yarn, then catch in the stitches to their correct place before sewing in the yarn end with a few more backstitches. Ensure that the repair is correctly tensioned as you sew.

may seem disheartening advice, but if you're "in" to this sort of knitting you're hooked; and you will not want your knitting to contain obvious errors. My rule for mistakes is that only you should be aware of their whereabouts in the finished knitting and not anyone else who hasn't got a lot of time and the capacity for very close scrutiny!

How To Graft the Edging's Start and Finish Together

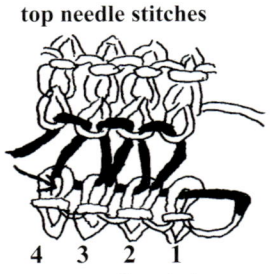

Grafting (Weaving – U.S.) is the technical name for producing by sewing, a join identical to a row of knitting. It is also known in one form as Kitchener Stitch. Make sure you have the same number of stitches on both sides of knitting to be joined. Keep both sets of stitches on the knitting needles – it's a useful tip to transfer both sets of stitches to a larger sized pair of needles to stop them slipping off so readily. You could also give a coat of spray starch to the stitches to help stop them unravelling. Thread a blunt tapestry needle with sufficient wool – about three times the length to be grafted.

Make sure your rows of knitting to be grafted resemble exactly the above drawing – knit (or purl) an extra row if necessary. N.B. The stitches are shown 'off the pins' for clarity. Keep them on the pin/needle until you have been through each stitch at least once. (Note, that apart from the first and last stitch, you go into every stitch loop *twice* before slipping it off the needle).

I give the **Garter Stitch Method for Grafting** here, refer to above diagram:

*On the bottom needle, sew *down* through the first stitch and *up* through the second stitch. Next, on the top needle, sew *up* through the first stitch and *down* through the second stitch. Withdraw the first stitches from both needles. Repeat from * (the second stitches on both needles have now become 'first stitches'). Regularly pull the sewing yarn through the stitches to lie in place.

Grafting, I think, is one of the hardest processes of knitting, but it is well worth practising and consulting the knitting reference books to achieve the desired best effects. You can evenly sew the borders together relatively loosely instead.

Dressing your shawl

Sew in any ends through lines of decreasing ('\'s) and dress the shawl by washing and rinsing it gently in luke-warm water and a wool detergent. DO NOT RUB, WRING OR CHANGE THE WATER TEMPERATURE AS THESE MAY CAUSE FELTING OR SHRINKAGE!

Use a clean, colourfast towel to wrap the shawl in, blot up the excess water till the shawl is damp but not dripping wet. Pull shawl gently to shape on a flat surface, pay special attention to the pulling out of each point of the edging. Now, using rustless pins and / or dressing wires – as below, pin so the shawl is a taut square – insert pins with the heads angled outwards to get maximum stretch. Leave till thoroughly dry away from heat or sunlight – I dry my shawls on the double bed; it takes them about 3 – 4 hours to dry, a cool electric fan in the room speeds things up a little.

USE PINS AND WIRES CAREFULLY, PROTECT OTHERS & PETS FROM PIN INJURIES!

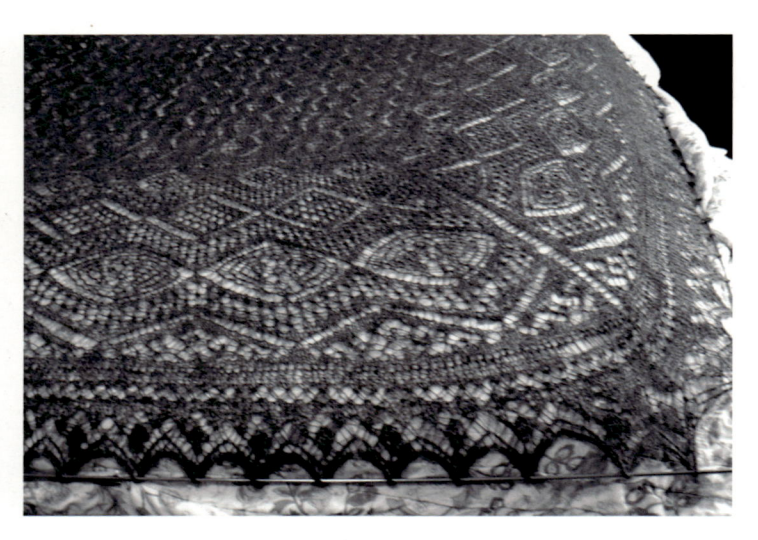